SKIMMING AND SCANNING TECHNIQUES

By Barbara N. Sherman

Published by Liberty University Press.
Printed in the U.S.A.

Liberty University Press
1971 University Blvd.
Lynchburg, VA 24515
www.Liberty.edu/LibertyUniversityPress

ISBN: 978-1-935986-66-9

First edition, August 2014

PUBLISHER'S ACKNOWLEDGEMENTS

A special thank you to all the individuals who assisted
in the creation of this publication:

Editorial Assistant: Arielle Bielicki
Project Editor: Leo Percer
Editorial Manager: Sarah Funderburke
Cover Art & Design: Glauco Lima & Jeremy McLemore

TABLE OF CONTENTS

SCANNING

DEDICATION

To my LORD and Savior and to my family

and

in memory of Dr. Jerry Falwell

"Let the words of my mouth and the meditation of my heart be acceptable in Thy sight, O LORD, my Strength and my Redeemer." Psalm 19:14 (KJV)

ACKNOWLEDGEMENTS:

First, for all the help and careful attention: Dixie Sanner and Canaan Suitt, and Grayson Sherman. I couldn't have done it without you!

Thank you to the following:
AlphaLists.com
Amtrak
Billy Graham Evangelistic Association
Liberty University Athletics Dept.
Liberty University Marketing Dept.
Lynchburg Parks/Recreation
Lynchburg Regional Chamber of Commerce — Lynchburg Life
Verizon

PREFACE

Welcome to this exciting worktext for enhancing your speed reading skills. Speed reading is an outstanding ability which can be mastered by anyone with practice and the proper tools. The author would like to recommend one particularly powerful program of brain enhancement technique which has proven overwhelmingly successful with thousands; the **eyeQ system** is available at the time of this publication as an online tool through which "we can significantly increase our brain's learning and processing ability through a series of high-speed imaging exercises which utilize both graphics and text."[1]

Two specific tools necessary for an effective regime of speed reading are **skimming** and **scanning** which have very different goals, reached with very different methods. Skimming purposes include a broad reading of materials, while scanning searches for specific information.

This text will provide introductory notes on each skill and then provide numerous exercises for practice in each. All are timed exercises, necessary for continued progress and measurement of improvement.

The skimming section has a decided historic, patriotic, and Christian flair, while the scanning section contains items of overall general public interest/activity. Answer keys are available at the end of each section.

Let's begin together!

---

1   http://eyeqadvantage.com/Personal/?gclid=CK6Di-qzzLkCFctxOgod8BIAQw

SKIMMING AND SCANNING INSTRUCTIONS

I.   You will need a reliable timer with a start and stop function and a sweeping second hand. You may also use a watch or clock with a sweeping second hand.

II. As you begin your reading, start the timer.

III. Stop the timer immediately at the end of your reading.

IV. In the worktext at the end of your reading activity, note the exact amount of time you read, i.e. 3:10 for three minutes, ten seconds. Do not include the time you spend writing your answers to the scanning exercises.

V.   Proceed to the scanning exercises, answering the questions as quickly as you can. You may look back, but try not to exceed five minutes in noting your answers.

VI. Use the Answer Key at the end of the section to grade your quiz.

VII. Comparative Ponderings: Compare your reading time and the time spent finding answers as you move through the section.

> Skimming: Your collateral work in eyeQ should allow you to move at an increasingly rapid pace through the Skimming exercises.

> Scanning: Scanning results will vary with the format of the item that you are scanning. For some students, directories are difficult while others may find schedules or tables more complicated.

VIII. In order to produce mastery of various reading formats, exercises and articles will be displayed in a variety of layouts.

SKIMMING

SKIMMING INTRODUCTION:

Skimming is a method of rapidly moving the eyes over text with the purpose of finding only the main ideas and a general overview of the content—some major facts may be absorbed as well.

I. Skimming is most useful in the following situations:
    A. Pre-reading—Skimming is more thorough than simply previewing and can give a more accurate picture of text that will be read fully at a later point.
    B. Reviewing—Skimming is a useful practice for reviewing text that has already been read/studied.
    C. Reading—Skimming is most often used for quickly reading materials which do not need more detailed attention.

II. Steps to Skimming an Article:
    A. Read the title—this presents the shortest summary of the article content.
    B. Read the introduction and/or the first paragraph.
    C. If the article has subheadings, read each of those, thinking quickly about possible relationships among them.
    D. Read the first sentence of each remaining paragraph.
        1. The main idea of many paragraphs is the first sentence; however, the following symbols indicate locations of varied topic sentence structures with the base line representing the topic sentence:

MAIN IDEA PATTERNS
(Base line represents topic sentence)

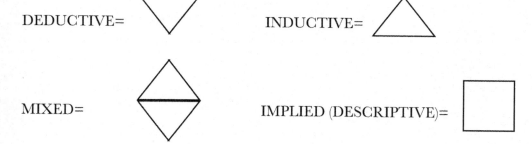

DEDUCTIVE=   INDUCTIVE=

MIXED=   IMPLIED (DESCRIPTIVE)=

        2. In the Implied Pattern, there is no one specific topic sentence.
        3. If the author's pattern includes using a question to begin a paragraph, the last paragraph may be valuable.

E. Search the text for the following:
1. Proper nouns
2. Unusual words, especially if capitalized
3. Clue words that answer Who, What, Where, When, Why, How
4. Qualifying adjectives such as best, worst, most, least, etc.
5. Enumerations (1, 2, or I, II, etc.)
6. Typographical clues such as italics, bolding, underlining, asterisks ***, etc.

F. Read the final paragraph completely.
G. Mastering skimming requires that you use it as frequently as possible.

NOTE: SKIMMING IS USUALLY ACCOMPLISHED AT 1000 WORDS PER MINUTE (WPM).

BILL OF RIGHTS

Start timer (or note time on clock) and begin reading as quickly as you can. Stop timer (or note time on clock) and record time in the box which follows the selection. Calculate time read and record.

Before the American Revolution, the original colonies were united under the Articles of Confederation, which did not address creation of a central (federal) government. So, in 1787, Founders called a Constitutional Convention in Philadelphia to build a structure for a new government. The resulting Constitution did not address the rights of individuals, which became a bone of contention during the ratification.

The provisions contained in the Bill of Rights were predated by the Magna Carta, which King John signed in 1215 to protect citizens against abuse of power by the King or Queen. Likewise, the authors (led by James Madison) sought to limit the role of the central government. Virginia's Declaration of Rights, drafted by George Mason immediately after independence in 1776, served as a model for other states' bills of rights as well as the first 10 amendments to the Constitution.

Once drafted, the Bill of Rights was quickly ratified by the states. It only took six months for nine states to say yes – two short of the total needed. On December 15, 1791, Virginia was the 11th state to ratify these 10, making them part of the Constitution. Two other amendments failed ratification.

Congress of the United States begun and held at the City of New-York, on Wednesday the fourth of March, one thousand seven hundred and eighty nine.

The Conventions of a number of the States, having at the time of their adopting the Constitution, expressed a desire, in order to prevent misconstruction or abuse of its powers, that further declaratory and restrictive clauses should be added: And as extending the ground of public confidence in the Government, will best ensure the beneficent ends of its institution.

RESOLVED by the Senate and House of Representatives of the United States of

America, in Congress assembled, two thirds of both Houses concurring, that the following Articles be proposed to the Legislatures of the several States, as amendments to the Constitution of the United States, all, or any of which Articles, when ratified by three fourths of the said Legislatures, to be valid to all intents and purposes, as part of the said Constitution; viz.

ARTICLES in addition to, and Amendment of the Constitution of the United States of America, proposed by Congress, and ratified by the Legislatures of the several States, pursuant to the fifth Article of the original Constitution.

Amendment I

Congress shall make no law respecting an establishment of religion, or prohibiting the free exercise thereof; or abridging the freedom of speech, or of the press; or the right of the people peaceably to assemble, and to petition the Government for a redress of grievances.

Amendment II

A well regulated Militia, being necessary to the security of a free State, the right of the people to keep and bear Arms, shall not be infringed.

Amendment III

No Soldier shall, in time of peace be quartered in any house, without the consent of the Owner, nor in time of war, but in a manner to be prescribed by law.

Amendment IV

The right of the people to be secure in their persons, houses, papers, and effects, against unreasonable searches and seizures, shall not be violated, and no Warrants shall issue, but upon probable cause, supported by Oath or affirmation, and particularly describing the place to be searched, and the persons or things to be seized.

Amendment V

No person shall be held to answer for a capital, or otherwise infamous crime, unless on a presentment or indictment of a Grand Jury, except in cases arising in the land or naval forces, or in the Militia, when in actual service in time of War or public danger; nor shall any person be subject for the same offence to be twice put in jeopardy of life or limb; nor shall be compelled in any criminal case to be a witness against himself, nor be deprived of life, liberty, or property, without due process of law; nor shall private property be taken for public use, without just compensation.

Amendment VI

In all criminal prosecutions, the accused shall enjoy the right to a speedy and public trial, by an impartial jury of the State and district wherein the crime shall have been committed, which district shall have been previously ascertained by law, and to be informed of the nature and cause of the accusation; to be confronted with the witnesses against him; to have compulsory process for obtaining witnesses in his favor, and to have the Assistance of Counsel for his defense.

Amendment VII

In Suits at common law, where the value in controversy shall exceed twenty dollars, the right of trial by jury shall be preserved, and no fact tried by a jury, shall be otherwise re-examined in any Court of the United States, than according to the rules of the common law.

Amendment VIII

Excessive bail shall not be required, nor excessive fines imposed, nor cruel and unusual punishments inflicted.

Amendment IX

The enumeration in the Constitution, of certain rights, shall not be construed to deny or disparage others retained by the people.

Amendment X

The powers not delegated to the United States by the Constitution, nor prohibited by it to the States, are reserved to the States respectively, or to the people.

Note: The capitalization and punctuation in this version are from the enrolled original of the Joint Resolution of Congress proposing the Bill of Rights, which is on permanent display in the Rotunda of the National Archives Building, Washington, D.C.

| START TIME: |
| END TIME: |
| TOTAL TIME: |

Page URL: http://www.archives.gov/exhibits/charters/bill_of_rights_transcript.html

U.S. National Archives & Records Administration

8601 Adelphi Road, College Park, MD, 20740-6001

1-86-NARA-NARA

1-866-372-6272

QUESTIONS ON THE BILL OF RIGHTS
Fill in the blanks with the correct answers.

1. Prior to the American Revolution, the original colonies were united under the

    _____.

2. The Constitution that came out of the Constitutional Convention did not address
    the rights of _____.

3. The Constitutional Convention was called in Philadelphia in _____.

4. In order to protect citizens' rights, the Founders used the_____,
    which contained such protection as a model.

5. _____was the eleventh state to ratify ten of the proposed
    amendments to the Constitution.

6. The right of the people to assemble freely is found in the _____
    Amendment.

7. The protection against unreasonable seizures is stated in the _____
    Amendment.

8. The _____ Amendment protects us from double jeopardy.

9. If we are criminally prosecuted, we have the right to a swift, public trial by jury as
    established in the _____Amendment.

10. Powers that are not relegated to the federal government or the state are reserved
    to the people as noted in the _____Amendment.

Check your answers by the answer key provided: Number correct_____
Record Selection Results:
1) Enter your reading speed on the Skimming WPM chart provided.
2) Enter your comprehension score on the Skimming WPM chart.

LINCOLN'S SECOND INAUGURAL ADDRESS (MARCH 4, 1864)

Start timer (or note time on clock) and begin reading as quickly as you can. Stop timer (or note time on clock) and record time in the box which follows the selection. Calculate time read and record.

Fellow-Countrymen:

At this second appearing to take the oath of the Presidential office there is less occasion for an extended address than there was at the first. Then a statement somewhat in detail of a course to be pursued seemed fitting and proper. Now, at the expiration of four years, during which public declarations have been constantly called forth on every point and phase of the great contest which still absorbs the attention and engrosses the energies of the nation, little that is new could be presented. The progress of our arms, upon which all else chiefly depends, is as well known to the public as to myself, and it is, I trust, reasonably satisfactory and encouraging to all. With high hope for the future, no prediction in regard to it is ventured.

On the occasion corresponding to this four years ago all thoughts were anxiously directed to an impending civil war. All dreaded it, all sought to avert it. While the inaugural address was being delivered from this place, devoted altogether to saving the Union without war, urgent agents were in the city seeking to destroy it without war—seeking to dissolve the Union and divide effects by negotiation. Both parties deprecated war, but one of them would make war rather than let the nation survive, and the other would accept war rather than let it perish, and the war came.

One-eighth of the whole population were colored slaves, not distributed generally over the Union, but localized in the southern part of it. These slaves constituted a peculiar and powerful interest. All knew that this interest was somehow the cause of the war. To strengthen, perpetuate, and extend this interest was the object for which the insurgents would rend the union even by war, while the Government claimed no right to do more than to restrict the territorial enlargement of it. Neither party expected for the war, the magnitude, or the duration, which it has already attained. Neither anticipated that the cause of the conflict might cease with, or even before the conflict itself should cease. Each looked for an easier triumph, and a result less fundamental and astounding. Both read the same Bible and pray to the same God, and each invokes His aid against the other. It may seem strange that any men should dare to ask a just God's assistance in wringing their bread from the sweat of other men's faces, but let us judge not, that we be not judged. The prayers of both could not be answered. That of neither has been answered fully. The Almighty has His own purposes. "Woe unto the world because of offenses; for it must needs be that offenses come, but woe to that man by whom the offense cometh." If we shall suppose that American slavery is one of those offenses which, in the providence of God, must needs come, but which, having continued through His appointed time, He now wills to remove, and that He gives to both North and South this terrible war as the woe due to those by whom the offense came, shall we discern therein any departure from those divine attributes which the believers in a living God always ascribe to Him? Fondly do we hope, fervently do we pray, that this mighty scourge of war may speedily pass away. Yet, if God wills that it continue until all the wealth piled by the bondsman's two hundred and fifty years of unrequited toil shall be sunk, and until every drop of blood drawn with the lash shall be paid by another drawn with the sword, as was said three thousand years ago, so still it must be said "the judgments of the Lord are true and righteous altogether."

With malice toward none, with charity for all, with firmness in the right as God gives us to see the right, let us strive on to finish the work we are in, to bind up the nation's wounds, to care for him who shall have borne the battle and for his widow and his orphan, to do all which may achieve and cherish a just and lasting peace among ourselves and with all nations.

START TIME:
END TIME:
TOTAL TIME:

QUESTIONS ON LINCOLN'S SECOND INAUGURAL ADDRESS
Fill in the blanks with the correct answers.

1. Lincoln refers to the Civil War as the great _____.

2. Regarding the Civil War, he said, "All dreaded it, all sought to _____it.

3. He refers to _____agents who were in Washington, trying to dissolve the Union.

4. "One-_____of the whole population were colored slaves."

5. The government claimed no more right than to restrict the _____ enlargement of slavery in the Union.

6. Lincoln noted that both sides in the conflict read the same _____ and prayed to the same God.

7. He urged, "Let us judge not, that we be not _____."

8. "The Almighty has His own _____."

9. Lincoln prayed that "this mighty _____of war may speedily pass away."

10. Perhaps the most famous line for Lincoln's Second Inaugural Address was "With malice toward none, with _____ for all."

Check your answers by the answer key provided: Number correct_____
Record Selection Results:
1) **Enter your reading speed on the Skimming WPM chart provided.**
2) **Enter your comprehension score on the Skimming WPM chart.**

"BLOOD, SWEAT, AND TEARS" BY WINSTON CHURCHILL

Start timer (or note time on clock) and begin reading as quickly as you can. Stop timer (or note time on clock) and record time in the box which follows the selection. Calculate time read and record.

The expression 'blood, sweat, and tears' is usually said to have been coined by Winston Churchill in his famous "I have nothing to offer but blood, toil, tears, and sweat" speech in 1940, when he warned the British people of the hardships to come fighting in WWII. However, it wasn't Churchill who coined 'blood, sweat, and tears;' ultimately it is has a biblical source.

KJV -Luke 22:44:

"And being in an agony He prayed more earnestly: and His sweat was as it were great drops of blood falling down to the ground."

I beg to move, that this House welcomes the formation of a Government representing the united and inflexible resolve of the nation to prosecute the war with Germany to a victorious conclusion.

On Friday evening last I received His Majesty's commission to form a new Administration. It as the evident wish and will of Parliament and the nation that this should be conceived on the broadest possible basis and that it should include all parties, both those who supported the late Government and also the parties of the Opposition. I have completed the most important part of this task. A War Cabinet has been formed of five Members, representing, with the Opposition Liberals, the unity of the nation. The three party Leaders have agreed to serve, either in the War Cabinet or in high executive office. The three Fighting Services have been filled. It was necessary that this should be done in one single day, on account of the extreme urgency and rigour of events. A number of other positions, key positions, were filled yesterday, and I am submitting a further list to His Majesty tonight. I hope to complete the appointment of the principal Ministers during tomorrow. The appointment of the other Ministers usually takes a little longer, but I trust that, when Parliament meets again, this part of my task will be completed, and that the administration will be complete in all respects.

I considered it in the public interest to suggest that the House should be summoned to meet today. Mr. Speaker agreed, and took the necessary steps, in accordance with the powers conferred upon him by the Resolution of the House. At the end of the proceedings today, the Adjournment of the House will be proposed until Tuesday, 21st May, with, of course, provision for earlier meeting, if need be. The business to be considered during that week will be notified to Members at the earliest opportunity. I now invite the House, by the Motion which stands in my name, to record its approval of the steps taken and to declare its confidence in the new Government.

To form an Administration of this scale and complexity is a serious undertaking in itself, but it must be remembered that we are in the preliminary stage of one of the greatest battles in history, that we are in action at many other points in Norway and in Holland, that we have to be prepared in the Mediterranean, that the air battle is continuous and that many preparations, such as have been indicated by my Hon. Friend below the Gangway, have to be made here at home. In this crisis I hope I may be pardoned if I do not address the House at any length today. I hope that any of my friends and colleagues, or former colleagues, who are affected by the political reconstruction, will make allowance, all allowance, for any lack of ceremony with which it has been necessary to act. I would say to the House, as I said to those who have joined this government: "I have nothing to offer but blood, toil, tears, and sweat."

We have before us an ordeal of the most grievous kind. We have before us many, many long months of struggle and of suffering. You ask, what is our policy? I can say: It is to wage war, by sea, land, and air, with all our might and with all the strength that God can give us; to wage war against a monstrous tyranny, never surpassed in the dark, lamentable catalogue of human crime. That is our policy. You ask, what is our aim?

I can answer in one word: It is victory, victory at all costs, victory in spite of all terror, victory, however long and hard the road may be; for without victory, there is no survival. Let that be realised; no survival for the British Empire, no survival for all that the British Empire has stood for, no survival for the urge and impulse of the ages, that mankind will move forward towards its goal. But I take up my task with buoyancy and hope. I feel sure that our cause will not be suffered to fail among men. At this time I feel entitled to claim the aid of all, and I say, "Come then, let us go forward together with our united strength."

| STAR TIME: |
| END TIME: |
| TOTAL TIME: |

QUESTIONS ON CHURCHILL'S "BLOOD, SWEAT, AND TEARS" SPEECH
Circle the correct answer for each question.

1. Churchill's purpose for this speech was to press the government to victoriously prosecute the war with _____.

    a. Italy

    b. France

    c. Germany

    d. Russia

2. A War Cabinet was formed of _____ members which would represent all factions of the nation.

    a. five

    b. ten

    c. four

    d. seven

3. Why did the positions for this Cabinet have to be filled suddenly in one day?

   a. FDR was visiting England and needed to collaborate.

   b. There was extreme urgency and rigour of events.

   c. The enemy was about to invade England.

   d. Churchill had set up a meeting with the enemy's leaders.

4. Who took the necessary steps to summon the House meeting?

   a. The Speaker

   b. Churchill, himself

   c. Neville Chamberlain

   d. His Majesty, the King

5. Churchill states that England was in the _____ of the_____.

   a. beginning… conflict

   b. commencement… most bloody conflict of human history

   c. outset… worst travesty of the modern world

   d. preliminary stage… greatest battle in history

6. Churchill offers his _____,_____, _____ and _____.

   a. toil, tears, sweat, blood

   b. life, liberty, happiness, honor

   c. blood, toil, tears, sweat

   d. tears, sweat, blood, toil

7. He declares that English faced what type of ordeal?

   a. "the most grievous kind"

   b. "a most tumultuous ordeal"

   c. "a divinely appointed ordeal"

   d. "a tortuous ordeal"

8. Churchill declares that the enemy is a(n)_____.

    a. great nation

    b. imperial nation

    c. former ally

    d. monstrous tyranny

9. Churchill stated that the greatest aim of England at that time was

    _____.

    a. victory

    b. conquest

    c. annihilation of the enemy

    d. assassination of the Fuhrer

10. Churchill calls for the aid of all in _____.

    a. fraternal affection

    b. imperial prerogative

    c. military support

    d. united strength

Check your answers by the answer key provided: Number correct_____
Record Selection Results:
1) Enter your reading speed on the Skimming WPM chart provided.
2) Enter your comprehension score on the Skimming WPM chart.

"WHY MY VOICE IS IMPORTANT" BY JONATHAN HART

Start timer (or note time on clock) and begin reading as quickly as you can. Stop timer (or note time on clock) and record time in the box which follows the selection. Calculate time read and record.

The story of history has been assigned numerous analogies by poetic historians. It has been described as an inexorable river, or a growing tree, or a winding road, but perhaps another metaphor that ought to be assigned to this list is that of a song. History may be viewed as a song, swelling and receding, soaring and falling, drawing to a climax and fading into a quiet that is no less important. It is we who provide the soul-stirring melody, the impossibly beautiful harmony, and the clash of dissonance that drives the music onward. Now, how is this achieved? In the midst of all this grandeur, how could we hope to make a difference? Perhaps more importantly, why should we even want to? To be able to answer this question, we must study history; we must understand how the song is played.

To begin, let us examine the melody sung by the heroes, the great leaders. Think of Julius Caesar, or Alexander the Great, or Henry V. What made these men's voices matter? Why do we remember the part they played? We remember them because they made a difference, because of their achievements. Now, think of how they accomplished their respective victories. Reflect upon the fact that a leader is nothing without those whom he inspires. Alexander would not have been Great without an army adventurous enough to follow his designs, without men who rose from citizens of a small Greek city-state to grand and noble soldiers conquering worlds that before had been unknown to them. Caesar's legionnaires, similarly, walked the same ground he did. They conquered every inch of ground that Caesar did, whether we remember their names or not. In other words, the common man can rise to and participate in the same sort of excellence that seems superhuman. In the heat of action, physical or otherwise, the social standing of a man does not change the greatness of his deeds.

As Shakespeare immortalized, Henry V led a small army of English peasants against an overwhelmingly large force of French nobles and high-born knights at Agincourt. They were exhausted, and starving, and soaked to the bone, and watched as the grand and glorious armored Frenchmen unfurled their banners across the sky. They were peasants on a foreign field fighting foreign enemies, and they were scared. They felt small. But they fought, and they won. Against all odds, they stood up for truth and were granted victory. These, the peasants, stood with their king in victory, and Shakespeare recounts that he hailed them: "We few, we happy few, we band of brothers." For they were brothers to him. They bled with him and cried out with him and stood with him, and in the midst of the action all of their voices mattered. The voice of the peasant rose with the voice of the king's, and each stood for truth and won the day.

With all this in mind, a suitable question would be: how do I make my voice matter most? In answering this we would again look back on those whose voices we have heard, and see that it is when we, as humans, take our stand and let our voices ring out loudly and clearly for the truth that our voices matter most. It is in Caesar crossing the Rubicon, proclaiming that the "die had been cast", knowing that adversity would come, and knowing just as steadfastly that he would stand for truth through it. He did just that. He stood for truth and he was cut down for it.

Our voices, our efforts, our striving, it all matters because every decision, every speech, every word, is either a melody or a harmony. Each one can stand for truth, and neither changes the music more than the other when they are united in purpose, when each stands for what must be said. It is possible to make a difference, but one should wish to transform the world, one should desire to shape it with your own action, because there is truth that must be stood for, and your voice can stand for it. Socrates, the great philosopher, said: "It is not living that matters, but living rightly." Merely generating noise is not enough. Every time you lead the melody, every time you support it in harmony, and every time you must clash against that which you know to be wrong, you are making your voice matter, and nothing, not the senators who stabbed Caesar, nor the French nobles who rode in insolence against the English peasantry, nor a friend chastising you for doing something that "wasn't cool" even though you knew it was right, can undo that truth or silence you from saying it. Your voice matters because it can speak truth, and that truth cannot be silenced by arms, or words, or even time itself. Your voice matters because it can be the proclaimer of truth with all men throughout history. Your voice matters because truth rings in its every note, and the final song is beautiful.

```
START TIME:
END TIME:
TOTAL TIME:
```

Author: Jonathan Hart, a student at New Covenant Schools (a Classical, Christian school in Lynchburg, VA).

Title: "Why My Voice Is Important"

Context: Optimist International Oratorical Contest

Purpose: The contest is designed for youth to gain experience in public speaking and provide them with the opportunity to compete for a college scholarship.

QUESTIONS ON
"WHY MY VOICE IS IMPORTANT"
Fill in the blanks with the correct answers.

1. The author's preferred metaphor for the story of history is "that of a _____."

2. An interesting reflection on leadership is "that a leader is _____ without those whom he inspires."

3. "Alexander would not have been _____ without an army adventurous enough to follow his designs…"

4. The author believes that the common man can "rise up and participate in the same sort of excellence that seems _____."

5. Henry V was the leader of a small army of English peasants who fought against overwhelming French forces composed of nobles and high-born knights at _____.

6. Henry's encouragement to his troops was forever remembered: "We few, we happy few, we band of _____."

7. The author believes that to make his individual voice heard, he needs to look _____.

8. Caesar marched forwarded steadfastly, the author notes, to the crossing of the _____.

9. His famous quote at that point was that "the _____had been cast."

10. "Your voice matters because it can be the _____ of truth with all men throughout history."

Check your answers by the answer key provided: Number correct____

Record Selection Results:
1) Enter your reading speed on the Skimming WPM chart provided.
2) Enter your comprehension score on the Skimming WPM chart.

BILLY GRAHAM: PASTOR TO PRESIDENTS BY JANET CHISMAR

Start timer (or note time on clock) and begin reading as quickly as you can. Stop timer (or note time on clock) and record time in the box which follows the selection. Calculate time read and record.

February 19, 2012 - Every U.S. President since World War II has met with Billy Graham. Both Johnson and Nixon, the two who probably sought him the most, offered him high positions in government — which he quickly and politely refused.

Billy Graham has often said, "Whether the story of Christ is told in a huge stadium, across the desk of a powerful leader, or shared with a golfing companion, it satisfies a common hunger. All over the world, whenever I meet people face-to-face, I am made aware of this personal need among the famous and successful, as well as the lonely and obscure."

Every U.S. President since World War II through Barack Obama has met with Billy Graham. Here are short snippets of their stories:

Harry S. Truman — In 1950 a congressman called Billy and asked, "Would you like to meet the President?" Without any briefing on protocol, he agreed and went in with three colleagues and spoke with President Truman, who told Billy he lived by the Sermon on the Mount. Before he left, the two prayed together. Years later, Truman warmly received Billy at his home in Independence, Missouri.

Dwight D. Eisenhower — "Eisenhower was the first President that really asked my counsel in depth when he was sending troops into Little Rock," said Mr. Graham. Just before Eisenhower died, Billy was invited to see him at Walter Reed Hospital. After talking again about assurance of salvation, the two men prayed. Eisenhower then said he was ready to die.

"Billy Graham is one of the best ambassadors our country has but he told me, 'I am an ambassador

of heaven.'" — Dwight D. Eisenhower

John F. Kennedy — Four days before he was inaugurated as President, John Kennedy invited Mr. Graham to spend the day with him in Palm Beach. "We drove around in JFK's white Lincoln convertible," said Billy. "During our conversations, I became aware that he was concerned about the moral and spiritual condition of the nation." During Kennedy's funeral service in the Capitol rotunda, Billy stood about 30 feet from Mrs. Kennedy and the family, and thought about the brevity of life and how people must prepare to meet God.

Lyndon B. Johnson — There was a religious side to Lyndon Johnson that people did not know. Billy was probably closer to Johnson than to any other President. He was invited to the family ranch several times and spent more than 20 nights at the White House during Johnson's administration. Every time Billy would say to him, "Let's have a prayer," the President would get on his knees to pray.

"My mind went back to those lonely occasions at the White House when your friendship helped to sustain a President in an hour of trial."

— Lyndon Johnson in a letter
to Billy Graham

Richard M. Nixon — President Nixon and Billy had been personal friends since 1950. Nixon was a private and complex person, but beneath the surface, Billy found him to be warm and compassionate, quite different from popular caricatures. He was rooted in the teachings and prayers of his Quaker faith. Often he asked Billy to pray with him and read the Bible when he would visit. In the last year of Nixon's presidency, Billy did not get to see him. Someone on the White House later relayed that Nixon said, "Don't let Billy Graham near me, I don't want him tarred with Watergate."

Gerald R. Ford — Answering critics of his relationship with Billy, Gerald Ford said, "I've heard the comments from some sources that Billy mixes politics with religion. I never felt that and I don't think that thousands and thousands of people who listen to him felt that. Billy dropped by the Oval Office on several occasions while I was President. They were get-togethers of old friends. They had no political or other significance."

Jimmy Carter — "Billy and Ruth Graham have been to visit us both in the governor's mansion in Georgia and in the White House," said Jimmy Carter. "His reputation is above reproach or suspicion." Back in 1966, Carter chaired a **BGEA** film crusade in Americus, Ga., and when he was governor, served as an honorary chairman of the Atlanta Crusade.

Ronald W. Reagan — Billy met Ronald Reagan a year after he married Nancy. The two remained close friends. "I remember when Reagan was president of the Screen Actors Guild, a union leader, and a very strong Democrat," Billy said. On March 30, 1981, after the assassination attempt on President Reagan's life, Billy flew immediately to Washington, D.C., to comfort and pray with Mrs. Reagan, and do anything he could for the President.

"It was through Billy Graham that I found myself praying even more than on a daily basis ... and that in the position I held, that my prayers more and more were to give me the wisdom to make decisions that would serve God and be pleasing to Him." — Ronald Reagan

George H. W. Bush — Mr. Graham has said he found George H.W. Bush easy to talk to about spiritual issues, "easier than other Presidents I have met. He says straight out that he has received Christ as his Savior and that he is a born-again believer." Billy was with President and Barbara Bush at the White House in 1991, the night that the Gulf War began. "Billy Graham has been an inspiration in my life," said Bush.

"It is my firm belief that no one can be President ... without understanding the power of prayer, without faith. And Billy Graham helped me understand that."

William J. Clinton — President Clinton once recalled, "When I was a small boy, about 12 years old, Billy Graham came to Little Rock, Arkansas, to preach a Crusade." Mr. Graham would not agree to segregate the audience racially, which made an impression on the young boy. When he was governor of Arkansas, Bill Clinton joined Billy Graham at a Little Rock Crusade in 1989. Mr. Graham also visited Clinton in the Oval Office after he became President.

"Billy and Ruth Graham have practiced the ministry of ... being friends with Presidents of both parties ... always completely private, always completely genuine." — William J. Clinton

George W. Bush — In his 1999 campaign autobiography, "A Charge to Keep," George W. Bush said a turning point in his faith came during a private talk with Billy Graham along the coast of Maine in 1985. Graham's words planted the "mustard seed in my soul" that eventually led to a decision to "recommit my heart to Jesus Christ," he wrote.

Barack Obama — President Barack Obama visited Billy Graham at his

Montreat, N.C. home at the end of his weekend mountain vacation in April 2010. He is the first sitting president to meet with Graham at his home, where the two of them had a private prayer time and some conversation. A White House spokesman said that the president was "extraordinarily gratified that he (Mr. Graham) took the time to meet with him." Mr. Graham said he was pleased to have had the president visit his home.

```
START TIME:
END TIME:
TOTAL TIME:
```

QUESTIONS ON BILLY GRAHAM
Circle the correct answer for each question.

1. Billy Graham was closest to which President, spending over 20 nights during his White House tenure?

    a. John F. Kennedy
    b. Lyndon Johnson
    c. Jimmy Carter
    d. Ronald Reagan

2. Which President was very fond of Graham but was rooted in the Quaker faith?

    a. Jimmy Carter
    b. Dwight Eisenhower
    c. Harry Truman
    d. Richard Nixon

3. Select the name of the President who was the only sitting President to visit Billy in his home.

    a. Barack Obama
    b. George H.W. Bush
    c. George W. Bush
    d. William Clinton

4. Which President, as a small boy, was impressed with Billy Graham?

    a. Harry Truman
    b. George W. Bush
    c. William Clinton
    d. Barack Obama

5. Which of the following Presidents offered Billy Graham a high government position?

    a. Lyndon Johnson
    b. Richard Nixon
    c. Gerald Ford
    d. a and b

6. What major act caused Billy to fly immediately to Washington, D.C.?

    a. Assassination attempt
    b. Declaration of War
    c. 9/11
    d. Impeachment threat

7. Which President did Billy go to see in the hospital shortly before his death?

    a. Richard Nixon
    b. Dwight Eisenhower
    c. Harry Truman
    d. Gerald Ford

8. The President who gave Billy Graham credit for a turning point in his faith during a private talk was…

    a. George H.W. Bush

    b. Richard Nixon

    c. Barack Obama

    d. George W. Bush

9. The President who claimed that his prayers for his decision-making were due to Billy's influence was…

    a. Dwight Eisenhower

    b. Richard Nixon

    c. Ronald Reagan

    d. George H.W. Bush

10. Bill Graham said that the President who was easiest to talk to about spiritual issues because of his forthright claim to being a born-again believer was which one?

    a. George W. Bush

    b. William Clinton

    c. Jimmy Carter

    d. George H.W. Bush

Check your answers by the answer key provided: Number correct____

Record Selection Results:
1) Enter your reading speed on the Skimming WPM chart provided.
2) Enter your comprehension score on the Skimming WPM chart.

WHY THE REVOLUTION WORKED BY MIKE KONRAD

Start timer (or note time on clock) and begin reading as quickly as you can. Stop timer (or note time on clock) and record time in the box which follows the selection. Calculate time read and record.

If there is one extremely deceptive aspect of the American Revolution, it is that the Founding Fathers made revolution look easy. Since that fateful day, over two centuries ago, revolutions have ruffled across the globe, many claiming to follow in the ideals of the American Founders, or claiming to take their principles to a higher level. Almost none of them succeeded. None succeeded as fully. Quite often the result was a tyranny darker than the one overthrown.

So why did the American Revolution succeed so wonderfully?

Four things are necessary for a successful revolution:

1) The old order must be rotten
2) The revolutionary cause must offer improvement
3) Circumstances must be providential

4) The revolutionaries must be worthy

The first requirement is quite often easy to meet. As a general rule, governments are rotten. Some more than others: but it is the rare nation that is blessed with good government. The question is: Is the government rotten enough to merit a struggle, particularly an armed one?

In the case of the American Revolution, the British government was rotten and corrupt to the core. Our school books dumb down the cause to mere taxes, but it is more than that. British laws had put a stranglehold on the American economy, with the intent of making America nothing more than a dumping ground for British manufacturers. Trade with the French or Spanish was forbidden.

To the untutored this may seem like nothing more than a protectionist policy; but in the seventeenth century this policy had reduced Scotland to poverty and Ireland to a slavish, starving state of penury; all by design. The rest of the Empire existed only to make London rich. On top of all of this, the colonists had no representation in the Parliament to correct the matter. Not that it would have mattered much with such a corrupt legislature.

Franklin, who had spent some time in the British Isles, had seen the devastation wrought by these policies.

Franklin toured Ireland in 1771 and was astounded and moved by the level of poverty he saw there. Ireland was under the trade regulations and laws of England, which affected the Irish economy, and Franklin feared that America could suffer the same plight if Britain's exploitation of the colonies continued.

More than anything else, Franklin saw how London Bankers, through the Currency Act, forced American colonies to stop issuing their own currency; and required them to take loans at interest. This caused an immediate depression in the colonies.

Franklin saw corruption and influence peddling that sickened him. He knew that America was slated to become nothing more than England's useful doormat.

Franklin had gone to England in 1757 as a cheerleader for the British Empire. He would return to the colonies in 1775 as a revolutionary.

The American Revolution met the first requirement. The old order was rotten.

The second requirement is to offer improvement.

One would be surprised how many revolutions do not. Quite often governments can be overthrown merely to exchange power, not improve the situation. This or that tribe feels oppressed, and overthrows the ruling tribe; but no improvement is sought. The underclass and ruling class have merely exchanged places. This is quite typical in the Arab and African world. The present Syrian Civil War between Sunni and Shia is just such a struggle. No matter who wins, the object is to oppress the other side.

In other cases, governments can be overthrown to prevent improvement. This is quite common in Latin America where right or left wing groups have been known to overthrow governments rather than have them proceed with reform. In such cases, the maintenance of tyranny is sought.

In Europe, governments were overthrown to institute murderous totalitarian regimes far worse than the previous order: often in the name of class or ethnic struggle.

In all these cases, these countries would have been better without such revolutions, if only to prevent unnecessary bloodshed, and quite often to prevent a genuine horror.

The second requirement of improvement is rarely met. The Belgians met it in 1830, but just barely. The French Revolution met this requirement initially, but then descended into the Reign of Terror – perhaps as a reaction against foreign interference. But the French Revolution became a bloodbath. Its initially high principles were trashed.

In America, however, the colonists had a clear vision of liberty; and what it meant. They had enough experience with self-government to know that they could indeed run things better than the British. They had been schooled in the writings of Locke to know how a good government should be framed.

The third requirement is circumstance. There are many fine, worthy people who have never achieved independence and liberty for lack of providential circumstance.

The Basque come to mind. They are an industrious people who greatly outperform Spain proper. Their per capita output is equal to Germany's. In the Middle Ages, they had a wrested a degree of local autonomy from Spanish kings and ran their provinces like republics guided by the fueros (laws). Moreover, they were amazingly egalitarian with their women; always a sign of high civilization. Devoutly Christian, the Basque – mostly part of the forces fighting Franco – refused to embrace the communist atheism rampant in the Spanish Republican ranks; to, remained proudly Catholic.

After Franco's victory, it was the Basque country which regularly protested against his fascist rule The General Strike of 1947 being a famous example.

Yet, this noble people is stuck between France and Spain. They will almost certainly never rise above autonomy, though they certainly deserve more. Likewise, can anyone doubt that if it were not the circumstance of adjacent geography, all of Ireland would be free of British rule by now?

Americans of the Revolution were blessed with natural wealth, a century and a half of practice in colonial self-government, and a history of self-reliance when

Britain ignored the, as it did during their Cromwellian Civil War. Most of all, the three thousand miles between America and Britain was a game-changer.

America's circumstances were providentially blessed.

The fourth, and most important requirement, is the quality of men. Most revolutions are run by thugs or benighted intellectuals: Mussolini, Stalin, the Assads of Syria, etc. Worse yet, they often depend on illiterate masses following them.

The Americans of the Revolution were the most unique people in world history. Literate, self-reliant, and moral at levels that is hard for us to conceive of today. They were probably the most biblically educated people in world history. Even the unbelieving Tom Paine would frame his pamphlet, Common Sense, arguing for revolution based on the Old Testament passages.

Contrary to popular belief, America was not one-third revolutionary, one-third neutral, and one-third Tory. In actuality, ninety percent of the population was in favor of Independence, to some degree or another. The American people were of a rare caliber of excellence, unity, and character. When one looks at other revolutions in history, no one other people comes close.

Cromwell, who claimed to be setting up a Christian Commonwealth in 17th century Britain, dismissed the Parliament, and assumed the mantle of Lord Protector; which is a fancy name for dictator. A Protestant Ayatollah.

Washington, on the other hand refused a similar prospect when Army officers at Newburgh offered to deliver the new American government into his hands. He would not take the path of Caesar, Cromwell, or the subsequent Napoleon. The Europeans were so astounded by Washington's character that he would be honored by all as a giant of history, even in his lifetime; even by the British. Upon news of his death, Napoleon had the French navy fire volleys in his honor.

The American Revolution succeeded because of a unique set of providential circumstances and righteous men. But let us not delude ourselves. The present day American people are not up to their mettle, not in the least.

Mike Konrad is the pen name of an American who is neither Jewish, Latin, nor Arab. He runs a website, http://latinarabia.com/, where he discusses the subculture of Arabs in Latin America. He wishes his Spanish were better.

START TIME:
END TIME:
TOTAL TIME:

QUESTIONS ON WHY THE REVOLUTION WORKED

Write "True" or "False" in the blank for each question.

_____ 1. Franklin saw corruption through the Currency Act by the London Bankers.

_____ 2. Oppressive governments are always overthrown to aid improvement.

_____ 3. One of the fine groups of noble people who have never achieved full independence would be the Basque peoples who are stuck between France and Spain.

_____ 4. The Reign of Terror in the Irish homeland was a reaction to foreign interference.

_____ 5. Franklin feared for the American cause as he had seen firsthand how Irish poverty had grown under British trade regulations and the laws of England.

_____ 6. One of the four things responsible for the success of the American Revolution was the revolutionaries were worthy men, not thugs or benighted intellectuals.

_____ 7. Egalitarian treatment of women is the sign of a deteriorating society.

_____ 8. One of the lesser known causes of the American Revolution was the strangle-hold of British laws on the American economy.

_____ 9. Franklin went to English in 1757 as a cheerleader for the British Empire but returned in 1775 as a revolutionary.

_____ 10. In the article, Oliver Cromwell is compared to a Protestant Ayatollah.

Check your answers by the answer key provided: Number correct_____

Record Selection Results:
1) Enter your reading speed on the Skimming WPM chart provided.
2) Enter your comprehension score on the Skimming WPM chart.

JOHN F. KENNEDY'S INAUGURAL SPEECH (JANUARY 20, 1961)

Start timer (or note time on clock) and begin reading as quickly as you can. Stop timer (or note time on clock) and record time in the box which follows the selection. Calculate time read and record.

Taking the Oath of Office, Washington, D.C.

_____

Vice President Johnson, Mr. Speaker, Mr. Chief Justice, President Eisenhower, Vice President Nixon, President Truman, reverend clergy, fellow citizens:

We observe today not a victory of party, but a celebration of freedom -- symbolizing an end, as well as a beginning -- signifying renewal, as well as change. For I have sworn before you and Almighty God the same solemn oath our forebears prescribed nearly a century and three-quarters ago.

The world is very different now. For man holds in his mortal hands the power to abolish all forms of human poverty and all forms of human life. And yet the same revolutionary beliefs for which our forebears fought are still at issue around the globe -- the belief that the rights of man come not from the generosity of the state, but from the hand of God.

We dare not forget today that we are the heirs of that first revolution. Let the word go forth from this time and place, to friend and foe alike, that the torch has been passed to a new generation of Americans -- born in this century, tempered by war, disciplined by a hard and bitter peace, proud of our ancient heritage, and unwilling to witness or permit the slow undoing of those human rights to which this nation has always been committed, and to which we are committed today at home and around the world.

Let every nation know, whether it wishes us well or ill, that we shall pay any price, bear any burden, meet any hardship, support any friend, oppose any foe, to assure the survival and the success of liberty. This much we pledge -- and more.

To those old allies whose cultural and spiritual origins we share, we pledge the loyalty of faithful friends. United there is little we cannot do in a host of cooperative ventures. Divided there is little we can do -- for we dare not meet a powerful challenge at odds and split asunder.

To those new states whom we welcome to the ranks of the free, we pledge our word that one form of colonial control shall not have passed away merely to be replaced by a far more iron tyranny. We shall not always expect to find them supporting our view. But we shall always hope to find them strongly supporting their own freedom -- and to remember that, in the past, those who foolishly sought power by riding the back of the tiger ended up inside.

To those people in the huts and villages of half the globe struggling to break the bonds of mass misery, we pledge our best efforts to help them help themselves, for whatever period is required -- not because the Communists may be doing it, not because we seek their votes, but because it is right. If a free society cannot help the many who are poor, it cannot save the few who are rich.

To our sister republics south of our border, we offer a special pledge: to convert our good words into good deeds, in a new alliance for progress, to assist free men and free governments in casting off the chains of poverty. But this peaceful revolution of hope cannot become the prey of hostile powers. Let all our neighbors know that we shall join with them to oppose aggression or subversion anywhere in the Americas. And let every other power know that this hemisphere intends to remain the master of its own house.

To that world assembly of sovereign states, the United Nations, our last best hope in an age where the instruments of war have far outpaced the instruments of peace, we renew our pledge of support -- to prevent it from becoming merely a forum for invective, to strengthen its shield of the new and the weak, and to enlarge the area in which its writ may run.

Finally, to those nations who would make themselves our adversary, we offer not a pledge but a request: that both sides begin anew the quest for peace, before the dark powers of destruction unleashed by science engulf all humanity in planned or accidental self-destruction.

We dare not tempt them with weakness. For only when our arms are sufficient beyond doubt can we be certain beyond doubt that they will never be employed. But neither can two great and powerful groups of nations take comfort from our present course -- both sides overburdened by the cost of modern weapons, both rightly alarmed by the steady spread of the deadly atom, yet both racing to alter that uncertain balance of terror that stays the hand of mankind's final war.

So let us begin anew -- remembering on both sides that civility is not a sign of weakness, and sincerity is always subject to proof. Let us never negotiate out of fear, but let us never fear to negotiate.

Let both sides explore what problems unite us instead of belaboring those problems which divide us.

Let both sides, for the first time, formulate serious and precise proposals for the inspection and control of arms, and bring the absolute power to destroy other nations under the absolute control of all nations.

Let both sides seek to invoke the wonders of science instead of its terrors. Together let us explore the stars, conquer the deserts, eradicate disease, tap the ocean depths, and encourage the arts and commerce.

Let both sides unite to heed, in all corners of the earth, the command of Isaiah -- to "undo the heavy burdens, and [to] let the oppressed go free."[1]

And, if a beachhead of cooperation may push back the jungle of suspicion, let both sides join in creating a new endeavor -- not a new balance of power, but a new world of law -- where the strong are just, and the weak secure, and the peace preserved.

All this will not be finished in the first one hundred days. Nor will it be finished in the first one thousand days; nor in the life of this Administration; nor even perhaps in our lifetime on this planet. But let us begin.

In your hands, my fellow citizens, more than mine, will rest the final success or failure of our course. Since this country was founded, each generation of Americans has been summoned to give testimony to its national loyalty. The graves of young Americans who answered the call to service surround the globe.

Now the trumpet summons us again -- not as a call to bear arms, though arms we need -- not as a call to battle, though embattled we are -- but a call to bear the burden of a long twilight struggle, year in and year out, "rejoicing in hope; patient in tribulation,"[2] a struggle against the common enemies of man: tyranny, poverty, disease, and war itself.

Can we forge against these enemies a grand and global alliance, North and South, East and West, that can assure a more fruitful life for all mankind? Will you join in that historic effort?

In the long history of the world, only a few generations have been granted the role of defending freedom in its hour of maximum danger. I do not shrink from this responsibility -- I welcome it. I do not believe that any of us would exchange places with any other people or any other generation. The energy, the faith, the devotion which we bring to this endeavor will light our country and all who serve it. And the glow from that fire can truly light the world.

And so, my fellow Americans, ask not what your country can do for you; ask what you can do for your country.

My fellow citizens of the world, ask not what America will do for you, but what together we can do for the freedom of man.

Finally, whether you are citizens of America or citizens of the world, ask of us here the same high standards of strength and sacrifice which we ask of you. With a good conscience our only sure reward, with history the final judge of our deeds, let us go forth to lead the land we love, asking His blessing and His help, but knowing that here on earth God's work must truly be our own.

STAR TIME:	
END TIME:	
TOTAL TIME:	

QUESTIONS ON JOHN F. KENNEDY'S INAUGURAL SPEECH (JANUARY 20, 1961)

Circle the correct answer for each question.

1. Kennedy described his speech as

   a. a celebration of freedom
   b. a victory of party
   c. a victory for all Americans
   d. a celebration of all citizens

2. To new states he declared: "…in the past, those who foolishly sought power by riding the back of the tiger ended…"

   a. up eaten alive."
   b. up thrown in the dust."
   c. up inside."
   d. up being the tiger's dinner."

3. He said that America wanted every other nation to know that America would do the following to assure the survival and success of liberty:

   a. pay any price
   b. bear any burden
   c. meet any hardship
   d. all of the above

4. He declared that two great and powerful groups of nations could not take comfort from their present course because of …

   a. "…the cold war."
   b. "…the refusal to agree to disarmament."
   c. "…the steady spread of the deadly atom…"
   d. "…disruptions in the Middle East."

5. For the sister republics south of our border, Kennedy promised "…that this hemisphere intends to remain the…"

   a. "master of its own fate."
   b. "master of its own future."
   c. "cooperating entity it is today."
   d. "master of its own house."

6. The first Scriptural quote Kennedy used was from the book of —

   a. Isaiah
   b. Jeremiah
   c. Revelation
   d. Ephesians

7. He declared that the trumpet was summoning Americans with a call, while "rejoicing in hope; patient in tribulation," to —

    a. a call to battle.
    b. a call to bear arms.
    c. bear the burden of a long struggle.
    d. a call to negotiate.

8. He felt that in the hands of his _____rather than in his would rest the final success or failure of the American course.

    a. voters
    b. political leaders
    c. fellow citizens
    d. advisors

9. His ultimate charge to his fellow Americans —

    a. " Ask not what your country can do for you but what your country needs."
    b. "Ask not what your country can do for you but what you can do for your country."
    c. "Ask not what your country has done but what it will do in the future."
    d. None of the above

10. His ultimate charge to the fellow citizens of the world —

    a. "Ask not what America will do for you but what you can do for America."
    b. "Ask not what you can do for America but what America can do for America."
    c. "Ask not what America will do for you, but what together we can do for the freedom of man."
    d. None of the above

Check your answers by the answer key provided: Number correct____

Record Selection Results:
1) Enter your reading speed on the Skimming WPM chart provided.
2) Enter your comprehension score on the Skimming WPM chart.

"THE ONLY THING WE HAVE TO FEAR IS FEAR ITSELF" FDR'S FIRST INAUGURAL ADDRESS

Start timer (or note time on clock) and begin reading as quickly as you can. Stop timer (or note time on clock) and record time in the box which follows the selection. Calculate time read and record.

I am certain that my fellow Americans expect that on my induction into the Presidency I will address them with a candor and a decision which the present situation of our people impel. This is preeminently the time to speak the truth, the whole truth, frankly and boldly. Nor need we shrink from honestly facing conditions in our country today. This great Nation will endure as it has endured, will revive and will prosper. So, first of all, let me assert my firm belief that the only thing we have to fear is fear itself — nameless, unreasoning, unjustified terror which paralyzes needed efforts to convert retreat into advance. In every dark hour of our national life a leadership of frankness and vigor has met with that understanding and support of the people themselves which is essential to victory. I am convinced that you will again give that support to leadership in these critical days.

In such a spirit on my part and on yours we face our common difficulties. They concern, thank God, only material things. Values have shrunken to fantastic levels; taxes have risen; our ability to pay has fallen; government of all kinds is faced by serious curtailment of income; the means of exchange are frozen in the currents of trade; the withered leaves of industrial enterprise lie on every side; farmers find no markets for their produce; the savings of many years in thousands of families are gone.

Yet our distress comes from no failure of substance. Plenty is at our doorstep, but a generous use of it languishes in the very sight of the supply. Primarily this is because the rulers of the exchange of mankind's goods have failed, through their own stubbornness and their own incompetence, have admitted their failure, and abdicated. Practices of the unscrupulous money changers stand indicted in the court of public opinion, rejected by the hearts and minds of men.

True they have tried, but their efforts have been cast in the pattern of an outworn tradition. Faced by failure of credit they have proposed only the lending of more money. They know only the rules of a generation of self-seekers. They have no vision, and when there is no vision the people perish.

The money changers have fled from their high seats in the temple of our civilization. We may now restore that temple to the ancient truths. The measure of the restoration lies in the extent to which we apply social values more noble than mere monetary profit.

Happiness lies not in the mere possession of money; it lies in the joy of achievement, in the thrill of creative effort. The joy and moral stimulation of work no longer must be forgotten in the mad chase of evanescent profits. These dark days will be worth all they cost us if they teach us that our true destiny is not to be ministered unto but to minister to ourselves and to our fellow men.

Recognition of the falsity of material wealth as the standard of success goes hand in hand with the abandonment of the false belief that public office and high political position are to be valued only by the standards of pride of place and personal profit... Small wonder that confidence languishes, for it thrives only on honesty, on honor, on the sacredness of obligations, on faithful protection, on unselfish performance; without them it cannot live.

Restoration calls, however, not for changes in ethics alone. This Nation asks for action, and action now.

Our greatest primary task is to put people to work. This is no unsolvable problem if we face it wisely and courageously. It can be accomplished in part by direct recruiting by the Government itself, treating the task as we would treat the emergency of a war, but at the same time, through this employment, accomplishing greatly needed projects to stimulate and reorganize the use of our natural resources.

Hand in hand with this we must frankly recognize the overbalance of population in our industrial centers and, by engaging on a national scale in a redistribution, endeavor to provide a better use of the land for those best fitted for the land. The task can be helped by definite efforts to raise the values of agricultural products and with this the power to purchase the output of our cities. It can be helped by preventing realistically the tragedy of the growing loss through foreclosure of our small homes and our farms. It can be helped by insistence that the Federal, State, and local governments act forthwith on the demand that their cost be drastically reduced. It can be helped by the unifying of relief activities which today are often scattered, uneconomical, and unequal. It can be helped by national planning for and supervision of all forms of transportation and of communications and other utilities which have a definitely public character. We must act and act quickly...

The basic thought that guides these specific means of national recovery is not narrowly nationalistic. It is the insistence, as a first consideration, upon the interdependence of the various elements in all parts of the United States — a recognition of the old and permanently important manifestation of the American spirit of the pioneer. It is the way to recovery. It is the immediate way. It is the strongest assurance that the recovery will endure.

In the field of world policy I would dedicate this Nation to the policy of the good neighbor — the neighbor who resolutely respects himself and, because he does so, respects the rights of others — the neighbor who respects his obligations and respects the sanctity of his agreements in and with a world of neighbors.

If I read the temper of our people correctly, we now realize as we have never realized before our interdependence on each other; that we cannot merely take but we must give as well; that if we are to go forward, we must move as a trained and loyal army willing to sacrifice for the good of a common discipline, because without such discipline no progress is made, no leadership becomes effective.

Our Constitution is so simple and practical that it is possible always to meet extraordinary needs by changes in emphasis and arrangement without loss of essential form. That is why our constitutional system has proved itself the most superbly enduring political mechanism the modern world has produced. It has met every stress of vast expansion of territory, of foreign wars, of bitter internal strife, and of world relations.

It is to be hoped that the normal balance of executive and legislative authority may be wholly adequate to meet the unprecedented task before us. But it may be that an unprecedented demand and need for undelayed action may call for temporary departure from that normal balance of public procedure.

I am prepared under my constitutional duty to recommend the measures that a stricken nation in the midst of a stricken world may require. These measures, or such other measures as the Congress may build out of its experience and wisdom, I shall seek, within my constitutional authority, to bring to speedy adoption.

But in the event that the Congress shall fail to take one of these two courses, and in the event that the national emergency is still critical, I shall not evade the clear course of duty that will then confront me. I shall ask the Congress for the one remaining instrument to meet the crisis — broad Executive power to wage a war against the emergency, as great as the power that would be given to me if we were in fact invaded by a foreign foe.

For the trust reposed in me I will return the courage and the devotion that befit the time. I can do no less.

We do not distrust the future of essential democracy. The people of the United States have not failed. In their need they have registered a mandate that they want direct, vigorous action. They have asked for discipline and direction under leadership. They have made me the present instrument of their wishes. In the spirit of the gift I take it.

In this dedication of a Nation we humbly ask the blessing of God. May He protect each and every one of us. May He guide me in the days to come.[1]

| START TIME: |
| END TIME: |
| TOTAL TIME: |

Source: Franklin D. Roosevelt, Inaugural Address, March 4, 1933, as published in Samuel Rosenman, ed., The Public Papers of Franklin D. Roosevelt, Volume Two: The Year of Crisis, 1933 (New York: Random House, 1938), 11-16.

QUESTIONS ON FDR'S "THE ONLY THING WE HAVE TO FEAR IS FEAR ITSELF" INAUGURAL SPEECH

Circle the correct answer.

1. Roosevelt stated in this speech that, "This is preeminently the time to speak the truth, the whole truth, frankly and _____."

   a. loudly

   b. patriotically

   c. boldly

   d. firmly

2. FDR compared industrial enterprise of the early 1930's to _____.

   a. rotten fruit

   b. frozen rivers

   c. withered leaves

   d. graveyards

3. To quote a Scripture, Roosevelt states that "...where there is no _____, the people perish."

   a. management

   b. leadership

   c. faith

   d. vision

4. FDR stated, "Restoration calls, however, not for changes in _____alone. This Nation asks for action, and action now."

   a. ethics

   b. government

   c. politics

   d. strategy

5. According to Roosevelt, America's greatest primary task is to _____.

   a. expose the Anarchists

   b. put people to work

   c. win the war with Germany

   d. subsidize American's farmers

6. To better use land, Roosevelt proposes "preventing realistically the tragedy of the growing loss through _____ _____."

   a. foreclosure on small homes and our farms

   b. forest fires

   c. the boll weevil's devastation

   d. hurricane damage

7. He mentions the _____
of all the parts of the United States and
recognition of the pioneer spirit.

   a. interdependence

   b. camaraderie

   c. allegiance

   d. power

8. According to FDR, our Constitution is
"...so simple and practical that it is possible always to meet extraordinary needs
by changes in _____
and arrangement without loss of essential
form."

   a. order

   b. voting

   c. emphasis

   d. structure

9. He forcefully stated that if Congress
failed to meet the nation's challenges, he
would request the use of _____

_____.

   a. Declaration of War

   b. extended Presidential power

   c. power to dissolve the Supreme
      Court

   d. broad Executive Power

10. FDR's concept of "the good
neighbor" policy meant—

   a. a nation which respects other
      nations first

   b. one that holds itself to a higher
      standard than its neighbors

   c. one that respects itself first in
      order to help others

   d. one that respects itself and the
      rights of others

**Check your answers by the answer
key provided: Number correct____**

**Record Selection Results:
1) Enter your reading speed on the
Skimming WPM chart provided.
2) Enter your comprehension score
on the Skimming WPM chart.**

HABITS AND ATTITUDES VS. TIME BY DIXIE SANNER

Start timer (or note time on clock) and begin reading as quickly as you can. Stop timer (or note time on clock) and record time in the box which follows the selection. Calculate time read and record.

We all face a daily dilemma — too much to do and not enough time in which to do it. Time management is the way we resolve that dilemma. The limiting factor is time — not activities. We need to make tough choices about what to do and what not to do.

Time is the limiting factor, not activities. If time seems to be out of control, then We are out of control and we need to learn more appropriate habits.

Proverbs 25:28 Like a city whose walls are broken down is a man who lacks self-control.

Even though city walls restricted the inhabitants' movements, people were happy to have them. Without walls, they would have been vulnerable to attack. Self-control limits us, but it is necessary. An out-of-control life is open to all sorts of enemy attack. Think of self-control as a wall for defense and protection against interruptions, distractions, gossip, temptations, etc.

The key to good time management is developing good habits. Good results come from good habits. Poor results come from poor habits. Although time is not adaptable, people are.

For our time management purposes, what's important to know about habits is that they constitute learned behavior. This means habits can be changed, that good habits can replace poor ones. Our habits may control our destiny, but we can control our habits.

Before we change our habits, we need to change our thinking. As Henry Ford said, "Whether you think you can or you can't, you're right."

We usually act in ways that are consistent with our beliefs. To become master of our time, we must start by believing we can do it.

How much do you really want to change your habits? Desire is the key to success or failure. No one can make you change.

How long does it take to change a habit? If you *consistently* practice the new behavior for 21 days, on day 22 it becomes automatic. You have replaced an old habit with a new one.

6 STEPS TO BETTER HABITS

1. **Identify the habit you want to change.** The more you know about what you do, when you do it, and why you do it, the easier it will be to identify bad habits. You will need to analyze your behaviors and where they occur.

2. **Carefully define the new habit you want to develop.** Write down what you want to change, and then describe the new habit you plan to use to replace it. Try to see yourself in the new role.

3. **Begin the new behavior as strongly as possible.** Tell others about your plan for a new habit. Develop a routine to go with the new habit. If possible, change your environment to help your new habit grow.

4. **Never deviate from the behavior until the new habit is firmly established.** Consistency and persistence are the only way to develop new habits. Part-time ap-

plication will not develop new habits.

5. **"Just this once won't matter."** The truth is every time you deviate from the new behavior, you have to start over again. The more times you attempt to start over, the harder it is to change.

6. **Ask other people to help you change.** Few of us make significant changes without the support of others. And above all, pray for God's strength and guidance.

Most important: Get started. DO IT NOW! Remember: *The short-term pain of discipline is worth the long-term disaster of the lack of it.* – Author unknown.

ATTITUDE

In our part of the world, most of us believe that being busy is a virtue. We feel guilty when things go undone. We want to do more, not less. We want to add, not subtract, activities from our lives.

The fact is: We can't do everything. Once we accept this, we've taken a big step toward becoming effective time managers. The key is having the discipline to concentrate on the *essentials* and eliminate the *non-essentials*.

Self-discipline and self-management — these are both critical aspects of time management. Our ability to control our time is directly related to our attitude toward controlling our environment.

Some psychologists divide people into two groups in terms of their attitudes toward their environment. They call them *internals* and *externals*.

Internals believe they can make a difference in their world and that they can control at least some of the things that happen to them.

Externals believe they are at the mercy of their environment and that they have no control or influence over the things that happen to them. They simply react to their environment, and usually whine and complain about what happens to them. Dr. Phil says, "Complainers are self-centered and immature. Their personal growth is restricted. And they typically have troubled relationships."

Proverbs 15:30 A cheerful look brings joy to the heart and good news gives health to the bones. We need to be aware of people with bad attitudes and not allow them to bring us down. Keep focusing on Christ and his goodness so we can pass along a genuine smile and hope.

The closer you are to the *internal* side, the more likely you are to gain control of your time. The closer you are to the *external* side, the more difficulty you experience with time. It will be harder for you to gain control of your time because you feel, deep down, that it's not possible.

The point here is, the more we BELIEVE we can control, the more we will TRY to control, thus, the more we WILL control.

Look at Jimmy Stewart's character, Charlie Anderson, in the movie *Shenandoah*. Soldiers had taken his youngest son. He and his other sons set off to find him. With very few clues, the task seemed impossible. When someone verbalized this to Charlie, he responded, "If we don't try, we don't do. And if we don't do, then why are we here on this earth?"

Remember: It's your *attitude*, not your aptitude that determines your *altitude*!

Excerpted from *The Master's Time Seminar.* SOS (Sanner Organizing Solutions) www.sos4order.com

STAR TIME:
END TIME:
TOTAL TIME:

QUESTIONS ON HABITS AND ATTITUDES VS. TIME
Circle the correct answer for each question or statement.

1. Too much to do, not enough time to do it. What is the limiting factor to this dilemma?

    a. activities

    b. time

    c. workload

2. What is the key to good time management?

    a. working more hours

    b. not taking vacations

    c. developing good habits

3. What is important to know about habits?

    a. once established, they cannot be changed

    b. we cannot substitute good habits for poor ones

    c. they constitute learned behavior

4. What determines success or failure in managing time?

    a. desire to change

    b. people making us change

    c. reading self-help books

5. How long does it take to change a habit?

    a. two months

    b. 21 days

    c. two weeks

6. What is required to develop a new habit?

    a. consistency and persistence

    b. doing it on your own

    c. take time to get started

7. What is an important fact to know about our attitude toward managing time?

    a. we can do what we put our mind to

    b. it doesn't really make a difference

    c. we can't do everything

8. Psychologists divide people into two groups in terms of their attitudes toward their environment:

    a. internals and externals

    b. doers and dreamers

    c. leaders and followers

9. You are more likely to gain control of your time if you are in what group?

    a. control freaks

    b. internals

    c. externals

10. What is it that determines your altitude in life?

    a. attitude

    b. aptitude

    c. both

Check your answers by the answer key provided: Number correct____

Record Selection Results:
1) Enter your reading speed on the Skimming WPM chart provided.
2) Enter your comprehension score on the Skimming WPM chart.

CHRISTIAN MISSIONS WORK IN ALASKA BY BRIAN TAYLOR

Start timer (or note time on clock) and begin reading as quickly as you can. Stop timer (or note time on clock) and record time in the box which follows the selection. Calculate time read and record.

The earliest mission efforts in Alaska began through the arrival of the Russians in the mid to late 18th century. The explorers first arrived with Vitus Bering around 1750 and soon began colonizing coastal areas in the Aleutians, Western Alaska, and Southern Alaska. The trade of furs boomed during this era, and the population of the Russian colonial villages grew, as well. Russian Orthodox priests followed this migration of colonists to the New World, and they began serving both the Russian colonists and the native Alaskans who had already been living in Alaska for centuries. Their work was primarily focused on the new colonial villages the Russians had established. Some priests ventured into isolated native lands and worked directly among the native people.

The best known of the Orthodox priests was Father Ioann Veniaminov. He first arrived in Alaska upon completion of his seminary studies around 1820. His primary purpose for coming to Alaska was to serve as a pastor of the Russian church in Unalaska, but he quickly began evangelistic work among the Aleuts of the region. He worked very closely with both Russian colonists and Aleuts, teaching them job skills along with the scriptures. He quickly learned the Aleut language, and he developed a written alphabet for the Aleut people. Later, he translated the Gospel of Matthew into the Aleut language, as well.

Veniaminov worked diligently to reach Eskimos and Athabaskans far outside of the Russian coastal colonies. Using traditional Native methods of travel, Veniaminov used the waterways of Alaska's coast to reach both coastal and inland native communities. His exploits in kayaking long distances became legendary among both the Native people and the Russians. In small Native villages and larger Russian colonial towns, he preached, taught, and carried out the traditional tasks of an Orthodox priest. Veniaminov trained Native people in the teachings of the Orthodox Church. He baptized large numbers of Native people, and he designed and guided the construction of many church facilities across Russian Alaska.

Veniaminov was very different from most Orthodox leaders in one key way. He took a strong stand in favor of allowing Natives to take a role in church leadership. He trained Native leaders, elders, and readers for the church, and these individuals helped the development and growth of the churches incredibly. In providing such leadership, Veniaminov helped open the door for native men to serve as missionaries, deacons, sub-deacons, and in other roles within the church. Through serving in a respectful way, leaders like Veniaminov helped the Orthodox Church become strongly established in many parts of Alaska, and this denomination's influence is still felt in many places in Alaska to this day.

Another example of the type of work done by the Russian Orthodox ministers in Alaska was the work of a monk named German. He arrived in Kodiak from Russia as a very young man, and he quickly became disillusioned with the Russians' overall treatment of the Native people. When he heard of the tragic deaths of some Aleuts who had traveled to meet with the czar (in order to protest against cruel treatment), German moved to a remote island off the Kodiak coast. There, for the next thirty years, he lived a life of isolation and prayer. Church leaders sent native boys to live with German and learn agriculture techniques from him. In return, he learned Native languages and of the conditions in which the Native people were living. During several different epidemics in Kodiak, German served the community as a doctor and helped both natives and Russians. His reputation grew after his death, and he was canonized as the first American saint of the Orthodox Church in 1970.

While men like German and Father Veniaminov did important mission work in parts of Alaska during the colonial period, overall, the church faced a difficult struggle during this era. The colonists tended to be very cruel toward Native people, with abundant stories of brutality. Additionally, many Russian colonists entered into many common-law relationships and unmarried relations with native women. Church leaders spoke out against such behavior, and in doing so, they came into open conflict with the Russian-American Company, a powerful branch of the czar's government that had been given the responsibility for administering the Alaska colony. In the end, the Russian church was able to bring a version of the Christian faith to many native people, but it was not effective in improving the lives of the Alaska native people in the face of challenging discrimination. Russian brutality definitely hindered the efforts of the Orthodox Church.

In addition to Russian Orthodox missionaries, Protestants also began mission efforts in Alaska very quickly after the arrival of the first Europeans in the mid-1700s. Among the early groups to travel to Alaska were representatives of the Moravian church. A small group of Moravian missionaries moved north in the 1870s, heading up the Kuskokwim River in southwest Alaska. Orthodox missionaries had begun working around the mouth of that river (the Bristol Bay region), but the Moravians went much further inland than the Russians had. This original group eventually established a mission in a region near several Native villages. They named their mission "Bethel." Their original mission activities made slow but steady progress over the years.

Despite tremendous struggles, the Moravian mission flourished. The missionaries struggled mightily with coming to terms with the Native culture. Edith Kilbuck, one of the missionaries, wrote of the difficult task of getting "the people to sufficiently understand the vileness of sin" and "to leave off from doing it." The missionaries in the Kuskokwim area also struggled against the power of the Native shamans. Yet another challenge was that of previous Orthodox teaching that some of the Eskimos had experienced. The Moravians did not shy from correcting false teaching, and they required that an individual have a salvation experience and testimony prior to accepting any Eskimo into full fellowship in their congregation. This was very different from the Russians. Despite the challenges they faced, this mission, and others like it in the interior regions of Alaska flourished, with many coming to Christ, schools being established, and eventually communities growing around these Christian congregations.

Sheldon Jackson's arrival in Alaska during the 1870s led to several improvements in Protestant mission efforts. He recruited ministers and missionaries from throughout the United States, and accompanied them to Alaska each summer. He assisted these ministers as they planted churches throughout Alaska, particularly in the southern and extreme northern regions.

Additionally, he worked among Christians of a variety of denominational groups. He organized mission efforts by a wide range of Protestant groups (Methodists and Baptists, in particular), hoping that by dividing the regions of the territory, larger areas could be reached in a more rapid pace.

After the arrival of Sheldon Jackson, Christian missions work expanded rapidly in Alaska. The Presbyterians established churches in the Inside Passage region and on the North Slope, while the Baptists and Methodists established congregations of believers throughout the rest of coastal Alaska. The Moravians did so in the Interior. The churches they established generally were organized and operated in a manner consistent with the churches of the rest of America. The buildings looked very much like other American churches, the preaching was of the same sort, and the music was generally made up of hymns, sung in English.

The importance of schools in the development of the church in Alaska cannot be overstated. Teachers are highly respected in Alaska Native culture, as are ministers. Native children quickly learned the English language and shared their knowledge with their families.

Local churches used this expanding knowledge to assist in Bible teaching. Basic English skills allowed for rudimentary instruction in Bible doctrines and some reading of the Scriptures in Native homes. These schools also served as the basic training ground for Alaska Natives to learn and prepare for leadership in Alaska's churches. Many men became lay leaders in their churches, while others served as pastors and evangelists in their home areas. Finally, many others have used the training they gained in these small village schools as a foundation for later learning in universities and seminaries elsewhere.

The establishment and growth of churches in Alaska has included a wide range of individuals from different backgrounds, strengths, and strategies. The work they have done has led to many coming to faith in Christ and growing in that faith. The work continues, as there are still many villages in Alaska that do not have any organized church of any Christian denomination or group.

| START TIME: |
| END TIME: |
| TOTAL TIME: |

QUESTIONS ON CHRISTIAN MISSIONS WORK IN ALASKA
Circle the correct answer for each question.

1. What Russian Orthodox priest first arrived to do missions work in Alaska around 1820?

   a. Dimitri Solznitch
   b. Vladimir Ovilinski
   c. Ioann Veniaminov
   d. Fyude Tolstoy

2. Initial evangelistic work was done among which people group?

   a. Lilliputians
   b. Commanches
   c. Aleuts
   d. Ents

3. What method of long distance travel did the missionary Veniaminov use that became legendary among the natives and the Russians?

   a. hot air balloon trips
   b. dog sled
   c. mule team
   d. kayaking

4. What sainted monk lived for thirty years as a recluse on Kodiak Island while ministering to local young men sent to train under him?

   a. German
   b. Ioann
   c. St. Michael
   d. St. Paul

5. What practice was condemned by the Church leaders?

   a. exporting native peoples to Russia for slave labor
   b. cruelty to native women and children
   c. Russian colonists entering into common-law marriages with natives
   d. both b and c

6. Besides Russian Orthodox missionaries, what other religious groups made an impact on the spiritual life of the Alaskans in the 1700's?

   a. Quakers
   b. Protestants
   c. Catholics
   d. Muslims

7. What was required for an Eskimo to be accepted into the established church?

    a. They had to pay a fee for a tithe.

    b. They had to provide five beaver pelts.

    c. They had to be baptized.

    d. They had to have had a salvation experience.

8. What mission group established churches in the Inside Passage region and on the Northern Slope?

    a. Presbyterians

    b. Baptists

    c. Huguenots

    d. Methodists

9. What was the organizational structure of the original churches in Alaska?

    a. Free choice of the individual congregations

    b. Similar to the rest of American churches

    c. Bishopric dictates

    d. Directions from the Pope

10. What language was taught to enhance basic Bible instruction?

    a. French

    b. Greek

    c. Russian

    d. English

Check your answers by the answer key provided: Number correct____

Record Selection Results:
1) Enter your reading speed on the Skimming WPM chart provided.
2) Enter your comprehension score on the Skimming WPM chart.

ASPECTS OF SPAIN BY DR. BRUCE K. BELL

Start timer (or note time on clock) and begin reading as quickly as you can. Stop timer (or note time on clock) and record time in the box which follows the selection. Calculate time read and record.

CONTROVERSY IN SPANISH BULLFIGHTING

Controversy surrounds one of the spectacles of modern Spain, the traditional *corrida de toros* or bullfight. During a recent EF College Study Tours trip to Spain, where I led a group of students, faculty, and staff from our university, we decided to attend an evening bullfight in Madrid, the largest bullfighting venue in that country. We were not unaware of the controversy that marks today's bullfights, but the tradition was too strong to ignore.

Bullfights in Spain start right on time, and so we hurried into La Plaza de Toros and took our assigned seats in the sun (less expensive than the better seats in the shade, but no one complained!). As the musicians played the traditional trumpet fanfare, the matadors and horsemen paraded around the large bullring, and the paseillo announced the beginning of the evening's festivities. Each bullfight consists of three parts, called *tercios* (thirds). In the first *tercio*, several bullfighters (that looked like junior varsity matadors, although I wouldn't want to call them that to their faces) waved their pink capes before the bull, causing the bull to charge them before they ran behind wooden barriers. At that point a picador on horseback entered the ring, carrying a long lance. The horse was protected by a covering that saved it from being disemboweled when the bull attacked the blindfolded animal. Meanwhile, as the bull had its horns caught in the protective covering, the picador used his lance to strike at the bull's neck muscles to further weaken the sweating animal. The trumpets then sounded to indicate the end of the first tercio.

The second *tercio* featured *la suerte de banderillas*, where three banderilleros sought to place colorful barbed sticks into the bull's neck muscles, a process that has the appearance of a ballet, as each man stood on his tiptoes and raced straight towards the bull. With the sticks hanging from the bull's neck, the third and final *tercio* began, again signaled by the trumpets. In this *suerte suprema*, the bullfight reached its climactic moment. The matador deftly waved his red cape before the charging bull, sidestepping the horns of the massive animal. Calmly, after several passes, the matador walked to an assistant and got the sword with which this final stage ended. The matador faced the bull, whose head hung low, and plunged the sword into the neck of the bull, piercing its heart and ending the fight. Each of the three bullfights we saw lasted approximately 25 minutes.

Clearly the controversy surrounding these bullfights involves the killing of the bulls, which PETA (People for the Ethical Treatment of Animals) calls a "tradition of tragedy" and a "ritualistic slaughter." In fact, Barcelona has declared itself "an anti-bullfighting city," and 38 Catalan municipalities have followed its lead in outlawing bullfights. This is not only a statement about the brutality of bullfighting but also an acknowledgement that soccer has surpassed bullfighting as Spain's #1 sport. This is also a political statement in that Catalonia wishes to distance itself from the rest of Spain.

On the other hand, a recent Huffington Post article states that Spain has taken a key step toward enshrining bullfighting as an acknowledged part of the nation's cultural heritage, a move that could "roll back the ban on the blood-soaked pageants in the northeastern region of Catalonia. Lawmakers in Parliament accepted a petition from bullfight supporters asking for the special status in a 180-40 vote that included 107 abstentions."

So we saw the bullfights and recognized the controversy. A number of us left the bullring impressed with the tradition, the pageantry, and the spectacle but also acknowledged that there is good reason for controversy. Now I'm going to pick up my dusty copy of Hemingway's Death in the *Afternoon* and re-read his account of this stirring but somewhat disturbing performance.

A UNIQUE STRUCTURE IN CÓRDOBA – THE MEZQUITA

Andalucía, the beautiful southern portion of Spain, is quite different from the northern parts of that country that include Barcelona and Madrid. This region is best known for cities such as Seville, Granada, Malaga (on the Costa del Sol), and Córdoba. EF College Study Tours offers a tour of Spain: Land of Many Cultures, and it's true that Andalucía contains a culture utterly unlike northern Spain.

Recognized by marvelous Islamic architecture, the region is rich in Moorish history. Local guides told us during our recent visit of the advance of Islam into Spain in 711 A.D., an important date to the people of that region. With beautiful palaces like the Alcazar in Seville and the Alhambra in Granada, the Moors spread throughout this region, and Andalucía was recognized for the peaceful coexistence of Christians, Jews, and Muslims for hundreds of years, but all that changed in 1492. The final push of the Reconquista that year expelled the Moors from Granada after an eight-month siege and ended the Moorish presence in Andalucía.

Among the most fascinating sites in all of Andalucía is in the city of Córdoba, not far from Seville. Described as "the most important monument of all the Western Islamic world," the Mezquita (or mosque) is the dominant item of interest in this city. Using pillars from the Romans, the Moors built and enlarged an enormous mosque, completing it in the 10th century with more than 1,000 pillars. The visitor today walks through a forest of these pillars with double arches of alternating red and white marble. Tour guides take visitors to the ornate mihrab, a niche in the wall that indicates the direction of Mecca, where Muslims faced during daily prayers.

After the expulsion of the Moors, a Christian cathedral was built in the middle of the Mesquita, removing approximately 150 of the pillars to construct the Christian place of worship. That construction would take 250 years to complete, adopting various architectural styles through the years, and today's visitor is overwhelmed by the anomaly of walking through a stunning mosque, only to turn into a gorgeous Gothic and Baroque cathedral.

A visit to Spain will reward anyone who travels there, but a tour of Andalucía is uniquely rewarding, since one encounters such different cultures, architecture, art, and food. Among the most captivating sites in that marvelous region of Spain is the Mezquita of Córdoba, a World Heritage site and a not-to-be-missed highlight.

| START TIME: |
| END TIME: |
| TOTAL TIME: |

QUESTIONS ON ASPECTS OF SPAIN
Circle the correct answer.

1. What does the author say about the controversy surrounding bullfights in Spain?

    a. He was unaware of any controversy

    b. He was not unaware of the controversy

    c. He says that there is no controversy

2. Seats in the sun in the Madrid bullring are

    a. More expensive than other seats

    b. Less expensive than other seats

    c. The same cost as all other seats

3. Each bullfight in Spain consists of how many parts?

    a. Three

    b. Five

    c. Ten

4. How is the picador recognized as he enters the bullring?

    a. He carries a pink cape

    b. He carries a red cape

    c. He carries a lance and rides on a horse

5. Each of the bullfights the author witnessed lasted approximately how long?

    a. About 25 minutes

    b. About one hour

    c. About two hours

6. The author of this article said he was going to re-read *Death in the Afternoon* by what famous writer?

    a. John Dos Passos

    b. F. Scott Fitzgerald

    c. Ernest Hemingway

7. Who has criticized bullfighting as a "tradition of tragedy" and a "ritualistic slaughter"?

    a. The Huffington Post

    b. The central government of Spain

    c. People for the Ethical Treatment of Animals

8. According to this article, what significant event occurred in 1492?

    a. The Spanish Civil War was concluded, with Ferdinand Franco taking power

    b. Spanish became the national language

    c. The Reconquista that expelled the Moors from Granada

9. The Mezquita in Córdoba is an enormous…

    a. sculpture of a horse and warrior

    b. mosque

    c. windmill that inspired the writer of Don Quixote

10. The beautiful southern portion of Spain is quite different from northern Spain and is called…

    a. Barcelona

    b. Andalucía

    c. Madrid

Check your answers by the answer key provided: Number correct____

Record Selection Results:
1) Enter your reading speed on the Skimming WPM chart provided.
2) Enter your comprehension score on the Skimming WPM chart.

MARTIN LUTHER KING'S "I HAVE A DREAM" SPEECH AUGUST 28, 1963

Start timer (or note time on clock) and begin reading as quickly as you can. Stop timer (or note time on clock) and record time in the box which follows the selection. Calculate time read and record.

I am happy to join with you today in what will go down in history as the greatest demonstration for freedom in the history of our nation.

Five score years ago, a great American, in whose symbolic shadow we stand signed the Emancipation Proclamation. This momentous decree came as a great beacon light of hope to millions of Negro slaves who had been seared in the flames of withering injustice. It came as a joyous daybreak to end the long night of captivity.

But one hundred years later, we must face the tragic fact that the Negro is still not free. One hundred years later, the life of the Negro is still sadly crippled by the manacles of segregation and the chains of discrimination. One hundred years later, the Negro lives on a lonely island of poverty in the midst of a vast ocean of material prosperity. One hundred years later, the Negro is still languishing in the corners of American society and finds himself an exile in his own land. So we have come here today to dramatize an appalling condition.

In a sense we have come to our nation's capital to cash a check. When the architects of our republic wrote the magnificent words of the Constitution and the Declaration of Independence, they were signing a promissory note to which every American was to fall heir. This note was a promise that all men would be guaranteed the inalienable rights of life, liberty, and the pursuit of happiness.

It is obvious today that America has defaulted on this promissory note insofar as her citizens of color are concerned. Instead of honoring this sacred obligation, America has given the Negro people a bad check which has come back marked "insufficient funds." But we refuse to believe that the bank of justice is bankrupt. We refuse to believe that there are insufficient funds in the great vaults of opportunity of this nation. So we have come to cash this check — a check that will give us upon demand the riches of freedom and the security of justice. We have also come to this hallowed spot to remind America of the fierce urgency of *now*. This is no time to engage in the luxury of cooling off or to take the tranquilizing drug of gradualism. Now is the time to rise from the dark and desolate valley of segregation to the sunlit path of racial justice. Now is the time to open the doors of opportunity to all of God's children. Now is the time to lift our nation from the quicksands of racial injustice to the solid rock of brotherhood.

It would be fatal for the nation to overlook the urgency of the moment and to underestimate the determination of the Negro. This sweltering summer of the Negro's legitimate discontent will not pass until there is an invigorating autumn of freedom and equality. Nineteen sixty-three is not an end, but a beginning. Those who hope that the Negro needed to blow off steam and will now be content will have a rude awakening if the nation returns to business as usual. There will be neither rest nor tranquility in America until the Negro is granted his citizenship rights. The whirlwinds of revolt will continue to shake the foundations of our nation until the bright day of justice emerges.

But there is something that I must say to my people who stand on the warm threshold which leads into the palace of justice. In the process of gaining our rightful place we must not be guilty of wrongful deeds. Let us not seek to satisfy our thirst for freedom by drinking from the cup of bitterness and hatred.

We must forever conduct our struggle on the high plane of dignity and discipline. We must not allow our creative protest to degenerate into physical violence. Again and again we must rise to the majestic heights of meeting physical force with soul force. The marvelous new militancy which has engulfed the Negro community must not lead us to distrust of all white people, for many of our white brothers, as evidenced by their presence here today, have come to realize that their destiny is tied up with our destiny and their freedom is inextricably bound to our freedom. We cannot walk alone.

And as we walk, we must make the pledge that we shall march ahead. We cannot turn back. There are those who are asking the devotees of civil rights, "When will you be satisfied?" We can never be satisfied as long as our bodies, heavy with the fatigue of travel, cannot gain lodging in the motels of the highways and the hotels of the cities. We cannot be satisfied as long as the Negro's basic mobility is from a smaller ghetto to a larger one. We can never be satisfied as long as a Negro in Mississippi cannot vote and a Negro in New York believes he has nothing for which to vote. No, no, we are not satisfied, and we will not be satisfied until justice rolls down like waters and righteousness like a mighty stream.

I am not unmindful that some of you have come here out of great trials and tribulations. Some of you have come fresh from narrow cells. Some of you have come from areas where your quest for freedom left you battered by the storms of persecution and staggered by the winds of police brutality. You have been the veterans of creative suffering. Continue to work with the faith that unearned suffering is redemptive.

Go back to Mississippi, go back to Alabama, go back to Georgia, go back to Louisiana, go back to the slums and ghettos of our northern cities, knowing that somehow this situation can and will be changed. Let us not wallow in the valley of despair.

I say to you today, my friends, that in spite of the difficulties and frustrations of the moment, I still have a dream. It is a dream deeply rooted in the American dream.

I have a dream that one day this nation will rise up and live out the true meaning of its creed: "We hold these truths to be self-evident: that all men are created equal."

I have a dream that one day on the red hills of Georgia the sons of former slaves and the sons of former slave owners will be able to sit down together at a table of brotherhood.

I have a dream that one day even the state of Mississippi, a desert state, sweltering with the heat of injustice and oppression, will be transformed into an oasis of freedom and justice.

I have a dream that my four children will one day live in a nation where they will not be judged by the color of their skin but by the content of their character.

I have a dream today.

I have a dream that one day the state of Alabama, whose governor's lips are presently dripping with the words of interposition and nullification, will be transformed into a situation where little black boys and black girls will be able to join hands with little white boys and white girls and walk together as sisters and brothers.

I have a dream today.

I have a dream that one day every valley shall be exalted, every hill and mountain shall be made low, the rough places will be made plain, and the crooked places will be made straight, and the glory of the Lord shall be revealed, and all flesh shall see it together.

This is our hope. This is the faith with which I return to the South. With this faith we will be able to hew out of the mountain of despair a stone of hope. With this faith we will be able to transform the jangling discords of our nation into a beautiful symphony of brotherhood. With this faith we will be able to work together, to pray together, to struggle together, to go to jail together, to stand up for freedom together, knowing that we will be free one day.

This will be the day when all of God's children will be able to sing with a new meaning, "My country, 'tis of thee, sweet land of liberty, of thee I sing. Land where my fathers died, land of the pilgrim's pride, from every mountainside, let freedom ring."

And if America is to be a great nation this must become true. So let freedom ring from the prodigious hilltops of New Hampshire. Let freedom ring from the mighty mountains of New York. Let freedom ring from the heightening Alleghenies of Pennsylvania!

Let freedom ring from the snowcapped Rockies of Colorado!

Let freedom ring from the curvaceous slopes of California!
But not only that; let freedom ring from Stone Mountain of Georgia!

Let freedom ring from Lookout Mountain of Tennessee!

Let freedom ring from every hill and molehill of Mississippi. From every mountain-side, let freedom ring.

And when this happens, when we allow freedom to ring, when we let it ring from every village and every hamlet, from every state and every city, we will be able to speed up that day when all of God's children, black men and white men, Jews and Gentiles, Protestants and Catholics, will be able to join hands and sing in the words of the old Negro spiritual, "Free at last! Free at last! Thank God Almighty, we are free at last!"

```
START TIME:
END TIME:
TOTAL TIME:
```

QUESTIONS ON MARTIN LUTHER KING'S "I HAVE A DREAM" SPEECH
Circle the correct answer for each question.

1. The King speech was delivered how many years after the Emancipation Proclamation was signed?

   a. 50
   b. 75
   c. 100
   d . 200

2. The "...great American in whose symbolic shadow we stand" refers to...

   a. Lincoln
   b. Washington
   c. Roosevelt
   d. George Washington Carver

3. Another analogy King used for "…we have come to our nation's capital to cash a check" was...

   a. "the debt owed to us"
   b. "..a promissory note to which every American was to fall heir."
   c. "the cost of our freedom"
   d. "guaranteed repayment"

4. "We cannot be satisfied as long as the Negro's basic mobility is from a smaller_____ to a larger one."

   a. ghetto
   b. cell
   c. farm
   d. cabin

5. " I have a dream that my four children will one day live in a nation where they will not be judged by the color of their skins but by the content of their _____."

    a. knowledge

    b. education

    c. character

    d. faith

6. "With this faith we will be able to transform the jangling discords of our nation into a beautiful symphony of _____."

    a. agreement

    b. brotherhood

    c. cohesiveness

    d. unity

7. "You have been the veterans of _____ suffering."

    a. creative

    b. horrible

    c. unimaginable

    d. unbelievable

8. "America has given the Negro people a bad check which has come back marked _____."

    a. overdue balance

    b. payment due

    c. partial payment

    d. insufficient funds

9. "This is not the time to engage in the luxury of cooling off or to take the tranquilizing drug of _____."

    a. acceptance

    b. denial

    c. gradualism

    d. waiting

10. "Free at last, free at last, thank God _____, we are free at last."

    a. our Father

    b. above

    c. and Son

    d. Almighty

Check your answers by the answer key provided: Number correct____

Record Selection Results:
1) Enter your reading speed on the Skimming WPM chart provided.
2) Enter your comprehension score on the Skimming WPM chart.

NINE THINGS TO LEARN FROM TROUBLE BY DR. JERRY FALWELL

Start timer (or note time on clock) and begin reading as quickly as you can. Stop timer (or note time on clock) and record time in the box which follows the selection. Calculate time read and record.

II Corinthians 4:4-18
(References are from the King James Version of the Bible)

INTRODUCTION

The book of II Corinthians is about trouble, Paul's physical weakness, and overcoming failure.

Principles of this sermon are for those who are facing a new marriage, a new business, or a new venture.

NINE THINGS TO LEARN FROM TROUBLE

1. We are just clay - we are not perfect, never have been perfect, and never will be perfect.

"We have this treasure in earthen vessels, that the excellency of the power may be of God, and not of us." (v. 7)

"Football is a game of mistakes; those who make the fewest mistakes, win."
(Sam Rutigliano)

Clay pots:

>   a. are never perfect,
>   b. will break,
>   c. will wear out,
>   d. are usually put aside for new and better ones.

Remember, we are clay. Therefore, expect trouble in your next venture.

Set a goal, aim at perfection.
Be realistic, accept imperfection.

If you have failed in the past, don't make excuses for your failure. If you make excuses, you re-establish the causes that made you fail in the first place.

Don't blame others for your failure. If you blame others, you gloss over the weaknesses that made you fail.

Don't blame circumstances for your failure. If you blame things, you blind yourself to: a. new paths to success, b. new friends who can help you succeed, and c. new ways to do things.

If you have failed, learn from Paul. "Forgetting those things which are behind... I press toward... the future." We have to always forget our failure and press towards perfection. But always realizing that we will never gain perfection.

If you are starting in a second marriage, realize that your mate will not be any more perfect than you are.

2. Life is a struggle - we must overcome our imperfections, overcome outward problems, and overcome circumstances.

"We are troubled on every side." (v. 9) The key to a successful life is to understand that troubles come to everyone - your parents, your teachers, your pastor, your friends, and to your spouse...

Troubles don't come from just one source. The Bible says they come from "every side." They come from church people, from your kids, from your boss, from the bank, from your spouse.

When you expect trouble, you have a correct view of life.

3. Make the choice that you will not go down.

The apostle Paul writes, "Persecuted, but not forsaken; cast down, but not destroyed." (v. 9) Life is a choice. You choose to be happy, or you choose to be a loner. You choose to be irritable or mad at everyone, or you choose to be a workaholic. People who are happy, optimistic, and positive, made a choice to be that way.

To begin again, you need to set a goal to be different. If you continue to live the way you were before failure, you will fail again. The attitudes that lead you to bankruptcy, will lead you to bankruptcy a second time. No amount of money will get you out of financial trouble, unless you change your attitude about life...

4. Be ready to be tested again.

Paul said, "For we which live are always ready to be delivered unto death for Jesus' sake." (v. 11) This means we are always ready to die or we always live on the edge of failure. Actually, successful people are just a step or two away from failure. In a race, there are usually just a few seconds between first and last place.

Don't fear failure, that is, if you have re-established new goals. If you don't make any changes and fail again, that is sad. If you make changes and establish new goals, but you still fail, that is not the end of the world. It just means that what you have tried does not work.

5. Develop a hope in the future and a love for tomorrow.

Paul said, "We having the same spirit of faith, according to as it is written, I believe, and therefore have I spoken; we also believe, and therefore speak." (v. 13)...

There are different kinds of faith in life:

      a. faith in God that leads to salvation and works miracles

      b. faith in yourself so that you know what you can do and can't do

      c. faith in tomorrow that gives you an optimistic point of view

      that God will help you through any difficulty that comes tomorrow.

Remember, there is no time with God. He is right now living in the "tomorrow."
He knows what is there, and is leading us into it. Therefore, let's trust Him and look
forward to tomorrow.

6. God wants you to be successful next time.

Paul has told us, "For all things are for your sakes, that the abundant grace might
through the thanksgiving of many rebound to the glory of God." (v. 15) God has
given us all things. He has given us eternal life, salvation, and His indwelling presence.
God has given us a relationship to Himself so that now we are His children. God
loves us as a father loves his child. Just as every father wants a child to grow and learn
the lessons of life, so God wants us to grow in every area of our lives and learn all the
lessons He has for us.

God wants us to be successful. It is not God's will that any of us fail, but rather that
all of us become triumphant. Then Paul said, "And thanks be unto God which always
causes us to triumph in Christ." (II Cor. 2:14)

7. Be willing to pay a price.

When we come to our next challenge, we must recognize that there is a price for every
victory. "For which cause we faint not, but though our outward man perish, yet the
inward man is renewed day by day." (II Cor. 4:16)

Everything in life has a price. When you win, you pay the price up front in practice,
discipline, and training. When you lose you pay the price afterwards in remorse,
embarrassment, and lack of achievement. When you see an educated lawyer, he has
paid the price by going through college and law school. He has jumped all of the
hurdles and answered all of the questions.

There is a price for success in every marriage. Both the husband and wife must pay the price. They must give up some of their selfishness and give up some of their privacy. They must pay the price of learning, talking, and sharing. There is a price in marriage and every successful marriage reflects both the man and woman who have paid that price.

If you have failed, there is a price to pay for success. You may have to sell everything and move. You may have to be re-trained and go to school. You may have to start at the bottom. You may have to move to another company.

If you have broken your marriage, you have to start over again. You have to find out where you are wrong, and change yourself. What is the price of a successful marriage? You have to meet the partner half-way. The man who is always right, and wants the wife to give in at all times, is completely wrong. The same thing goes for the woman.

8. Learn from failures.

Paul tells us, "For our light affliction, which is but for a moment, worketh for us a far more exceeding and eternal weight of glory." (v. 17) This means we should learn from our failures and be better.

I said a moment ago that there is a price for failure — remorse, regret, and shame. But there are other prices to pay, and the price can become a down payment or investment in learning a new lesson to never make that failure again.

There is nothing wrong with failure, but everything is wrong when we don't learn from our failures. Every child has probably fallen off of a bicycle trying to learn to ride. There is no embarrassment in that. But when you continue to fall off the bicycle for 20 years, there is something wrong...

9. Look beyond tomorrow to eternity.

Paul tells us, "We look not at the things that are seen, but at the things which are not seen; the things which are seen are temporal, but the things which are not seen are eternal." (v.18)

If you have failed, what you need to do is to look beyond circumstances and other people. Look to Jesus Christ. If you failed in business, next time take Jesus as a partner. If you failed in a relationship, next time make Jesus the primary One. If you failed in a marriage, next time make Jesus the center of the marriage.

Don't just look at being better, or learning lessons. Look all the way into heaven to Jesus Christ.

If you have never really accepted Jesus as your personal Savior, would you do it right now? Do not delay or put it off. If you would like to receive Christ by faith, pray this simple prayer in your heart:

Dear Lord, I acknowledge that I am a sinner. I believe Jesus died for my sins on the cross, and rose again the third day. I repent of my sins. By faith I receive the Lord Jesus as my Savior. You promised to save me, and I believe You, because You are God and cannot lie. I believe right now that the Lord Jesus is my personal Savior, and that all my sins are forgiven through His precious blood. I thank You, dear Lord, for saving me. In Jesus' name, Amen.

| START TIME: |
| END TIME: |
| TOTAL TIME: |

QUESTIONS ON NINE THINGS TO LEARN FROM TROUBLE
Write "True" or "False" in the blank for each question.

_____ 1. Troubles usually come from one main source.

_____ 2. To begin again, you need to set a goal to be different.

_____ 3. Develop a love for the future and a love for tomorrow.

_____ 4. There is a price for success in every marriage.

_____ 5. That price is in part giving up selfishness and privacy.

_____ 6. Look beyond tomorrow to your destiny in life.

_____ 7. Everything in life has a price; when you lose, you pay the price in remorse, embarrassment and lack of achievement.

_____ 8. Set your goals but be careful not to aim for perfection.

_____ 9. Blaming others for your failures will blind you to new paths to success.

_____ 10. When you expect trouble, you have a correct view of life.

Check your answers by the answer key provided: Number correct_____

Record Selection Results:
1) Enter your reading speed on the Skimming WPM chart provided.
2) Enter your comprehension score on the Skimming WPM chart.

RONALD REAGAN-MONTAGE: BEL AIR PRESBYTERIAN CHURCH

Start timer (or note time on clock) and begin reading as quickly as you can. Stop timer (or note time on clock) and record time in the box which follows the selection. Calculate time read and record.

Someone asked me whether I was aware of all the people out there who were praying for the President, and I had to say,

"Yes, I am; I have felt it; I believe in intercessory prayer, but I couldn't help but say to that questioner after that, if sometimes when he was praying, he got a busy signal, it was just me in there ahead of him!"

I think I understand how Abraham Lincoln felt when he said, "I have been driven many times to my knees by the overwhelming conviction that I had nowhere else to go."

Now I realize that it is fashionable in some circles to believe that no one in government should encourage others to read the Bible, that we are told we will violate the constitutional separation of church and state, established by the Founding Fathers in the First Amendment. The First Amendment was not written to protect people and their laws from religious values; it was written to protect those values from government tyranny.

I've said that we must be cautious in claiming that God is on our side. I think the real question we must answer is — are we on His side?

No matter where we live we have the promise that can make all the difference — a promise from Jesus to soothe our sorrows, heal our hearts, and drive away our fears. He promised there would not be a dark night that does not end. Our weeping may endure for a night, but joy cometh in the morning. He promised, if our hearts are true, His love will be as sure as sunlight. And by dying for us, Jesus showed us how far our love should be ready to go -- all the way: For God so loved the world that He gave His only begotten Son that whosoever believeth him in Him should not perish but have everlasting life.

America yearns to explore life's deepest truths and to say that their entertainment -- their idea of entertainment is sex and violence and crime -- is an insult to their goodness and intelligence. We are a people who believe love can triumph over hate, creativity over destruction and hope over despair. And that is why so many millions hunger for God's good news. I have always believed each of us was put here for a reason -- that there is a plan -- somehow a divine plan for all of us. I know now that whatever days are left for me belong to Him.

I also believe this blessed land was set apart in a very special way. Our forbearers came not for gold but mainly in search of God and the freedom to worship in their own way. We've been a free people living under the law with faith in our Maker and in our future. I have said before that the most sublime picture in American history is of George Washington on his knees in the snow at Valley Forge. That image personifies a people who know that it is not enough to depend upon our own courage and goodness. We must also seek help from God our Father and Preserver. We will never find every answer, solve every problem, or heal every wound. But we can do a lot if we walk together down that one path that we know provides real hope. The morality and value such faith implies are deeply imbedded in our national character. Our country embraces those principles by design and we abandon them at our peril. My experience in this office I hold has only deepened the belief I have held for many years. Within the covers of that single book are all the answers to all the problems that face us today if we would only read and believe.

America was founded by people who believe that God was their rock of safety. I recognize we must be cautious in claiming that God is on our side, but I think it's all right to keep asking if we're on His side.

I believe with all my heart that standing up for America means standing up for the God who has so blessed our land. We need God's help to guide our nation through stormy seas. But we can't expect Him to protect America in a crisis if we just leave

Him over on the shelf in our day-to-day living.

The time has come to turn to God and reassert our trust in Him for the healing of America – our country is in need of and ready for a spiritual renewal.

All great change in America begins at the dinner table.

America has begun a spiritual reawakening. Faith and hope are being restored.

Americans are turning back to God. Church attendance is up. Audiences for religious books and broadcasts are growing. And I do believe that He has begun to heal our blessed land.

"We believe faith and freedom must be our guiding stars, for they show us truth, they make us brave, give us hope, and leave us wiser than we were."

Of the four wars in my lifetime, none came about because the U.S. was too strong. Don't be afraid to see what you see.

Freedom is never more than one generation away from extinction. We didn't pass it to our children in the bloodstream. It must be fought for, protected, and handed on for them to do the same, or one day we will spend our sunset years telling our children and our children's children what it was once like in the United States where men were free.

I know in my heart that man is good. That what is right will always eventually triumph. And there's purpose and worth to each and every life.

Let us be sure that those who come after will say of us in our time, that in our time we did everything that could be done. We finished the race; we kept them free; we kept the faith.

No government ever voluntarily reduces itself in size. Government programs, once launched, never disappear. Actually, a government bureau is the nearest thing to eternal life we'll ever see on this earth!

There are no easy answers but there are simple answers. We must have the courage to do what we know is morally right.

We must reject the idea that every time a law's broken, society is guilty rather than the lawbreaker. It is time to restore the American precept that each individual is accountable for his actions.

Above all, we must realize that no arsenal, or no weapon in the arsenals of the world, is so formidable as the will and moral courage of free men and women. It is a weapon our adversaries in today's world do not have.

Without God, democracy will not and cannot long endure.

"The American dream is not that every man must be level with every other man. The American dream is that every man must be free to become whatever God intends he should become."

"I've spoken of the shining city all my political life, but I don't know if I ever quite communicated what I saw when I said it. But in my mind it was a tall proud city built on rocks stronger than oceans, wind-swept, God-blessed, and teeming with people of all kinds living in harmony and peace, a city with free ports that hummed with commerce and creativity, and if there had to be city walls, the walls had doors and the doors were open to anyone with the will and the heart to get here. That's how I saw it and see it still."

And how stands the city on this winter night? More prosperous, more secure, and happier than it was eight years ago. But more than that; after 200 years, two centuries, she still stands strong and true on the granite ridge, and her glow has held steady no matter what storm. And she's still a beacon, still a magnet for all who must have freedom, for all the pilgrims from all the lost places who are hurtling through the darkness, toward home."

———————————

10. "Some people wonder all their lives if they've made a difference. The Marines

don't have that problem."

9. "History teaches that war begins when governments believe the price of aggression is cheap."

8. "Freedom is never more than one generation away from extinction. We didn't pass it to our children in the bloodstream. It must be fought for, protected, and handed on for them to do the same, or one day we will spend our sunset years telling our children and our children's children what it was once like in the United States where men were free."

7. "Our people look for a cause to believe in. Is it a third party we need, or is it a new and revitalized second party, raising a banner of no pale pastels, but bold colors which make it unmistakably clear where we stand on all of the issues troubling the people?"

6. "Today we did what we had to do. They counted on America to be passive. They counted wrong."

5. "Of the four wars in my lifetime, none came about because the U.S. was too strong."

4. "Government's view of the economy could be summed up in a few short phrases: If it moves, tax it. If it keeps moving, regulate it. And if it stops moving, subsidize it."

3. "The nine most terrifying words in the English language are, 'I'm from the government and I'm here to help.'"

2. "We don't have a trillion-dollar debt because we haven't taxed enough; we have a trillion-dollar debt because we spend too much."

1. "General Secretary Gorbachev, if you seek peace, if you seek prosperity for the Soviet Union and Eastern Europe, if you seek liberalization: Come here to this gate! Mr. Gorbachev, open this gate! Mr. Gorbachev, tear down this wall."

Let us be sure that those who come after will say of us in our time, that in our time we did everything that could be done. We finished the race; we kept them free; we kept the faith.

| START TIME: |
| END TIME: |
| TOTAL TIME: |

QUESTIONS ON REAGAN MONTAGE
Write "True" or "False" in the blank for each question.

_____ 1. Reagan stated publicly that he believed in intercessory prayer for the President.

_____ 2. He identified with Lincoln who said that many times he had been "driven to my knees with the overwhelming conviction that I had nowhere else to go."

_____ 3. He declared that the First Amendment was written to protect the people and their laws from religious values.

_____ 4. He quoted the Scripture that "weeping may endure for a night, but joy cometh in the morning."

_____ 5. He believed that within the covers of the Bible were "all the answers to all the problems that face us today if we would only read and believe."

_____ 6. Freedom, according to Reagan, is always just two or three generations away from extinction.

_____ 7. Reagan believed that without voter involvement "democracy will not and cannot long endure."

_____ 8. His " 'shining city on a hill' was, in his own mind, one with open doors open to anyone with the will and the heart to get here."

_____ 9. He believed that we might need a third party, raising a banner of "no pale pastels."

_____ 10. Perhaps his most famous line was to Russia's General Secretary Gorbachev: "...Come here to this gate! Mr. Gorbachev, open this gate! Mr. Gorbachev, tear down this wall."

Check your answers by the answer key provided: Number correct____

Record Selection Results:
1) **Enter your reading speed on the Skimming WPM chart provided.**
2) **Enter your comprehension score on the Skimming WPM chart.**

SKIMMING ANSWER KEYS

1. Bill of Rights

1. Articles of Confederation   2. individuals   3. 1787   4. Magna Carta
5. Virginia   6. I   7. IV   8. V   9. VI   10. X

2. Lincoln, Second Inaugural Address

1. contest   2. avert   3. urgent   4. eighth   5. territorial   6. Bible   7. judged
8. purposes   9. scourge   10. charity

3. Churchill, Blood, Sweat, and Tears

1. c   2. a   3. b   4. a   5. d   6. c   7. a   8. d   9. a   10. d

4. Hart, Why My Voice Is Important

1. song   2. nothing   3. Great   4. superhuman   5. Agincourt   6. brothers
7. back   8. Rubicon   9. die   10. proclaimer

5. Billy Graham, Pastor to Presidents

1. b   2. d   3. a   4. c   5. d   6. a   7. b   8. d   9. c   10. d

6. M. Konrad, Why the Revolution Worked

1. True   2. False   3. True   4. False   5. True   6. True   7. False   8. False   9. True
10. True

7. J. F. Kennedy, Inaugural Address

1. a.   2. c   3. d   4. c   5. d   6. a   7. c   8. c   9. b   10. c

8. F. D. Roosevelt, The Only Thing We Have to Fear Is Fear Itself

1. c.   2. c   3. d   4. a   5. b   6. a   7. a   8. c   9. d   10. d

9. D. Sanner, Habits and Attitude Vs. Time

1. b.   2. c   3. c.   4. a   5. b   6. a   7. c   8. a   9. b   10. a

10. B. Taylor, Christian Missions Work in Alaska

1. c   2. c   3. d   4. a   5. d   6. b   7. d   8. a   9. b   10. d

11. B. Bell, Aspects of Spain

1. b.   2. b.   3. a.   4. c   5. a   6. c   7. c   8. c   9. b   10. b

12. M.L. King, I Have a Dream

1. c   2. a   3. b   4. a   5. c   6. b   7. a   8. d   9. c   10. d

13. Dr. Jerry Falwell, Nine Things to Learn from Trouble

1. False   2. True   3. False   4. True   5. True   6. False   7. True   8. False   9. True
10. True

14. R. Reagan, Reagan Montage

1. True   2. True   3. False   4. True   5. True   6. False   7. False   8. True   9. False
10. True

Directions: Skimming WPM Chart

Using the Skimming: Words Per Minute Chart, find the time closest to your previously noted skimming time for each article. In the columns under each article title, find the WPM skimming rate that corresponds to your noted skimming time for that specific article.

Minutes and Seconds	Bill of Rights	Lincoln's Second Inaugural Address	Churchill, Blood Sweat, Tears	J. Hart, Why My Voice Matters	Billy Graham, Pastor to Presidents	M. Konrad, Why the Revolution Worked	JFK Inaugural Speech
Words per Minute	932	702	759	894	1175	1350	1400
2:00	468	354	378	450	588	678	702
2:10	432	324	348	414	540	624	648
2:20	402	300	324	384	504	576	600
2:30	372	282	306	360	468	540	558
2:40	348	264	282	336	438	504	528
2:50	330	246	270	318	414	474	492
3:00	312	234	252	300	390	450	468
3:10	294	222	240	282	372	426	444
3:20	282	210	228	270	354	408	420
3:30	264	198	216	258	336	384	402
3:40	252	192	210	246	318	366	384
3:50	246	186	198	234	306	354	366
4:00	234	174	192	222	294	336	348
4:10	222	168	180	216	282	324	336
4:20	216	162	174	204	270	312	324
4:30	210	156	168	198	264	300	312
4:40	198	150	162	192	252	288	300
4:50	192	144	156	186	246	282	288
5:00	186	138	150	180	234	270	282

Minutes and Seconds	FDR Fear Itself	D.Sanner Habits vs. Time	B. Taylor, Christian Missions in Alaska	B.Bell, Aspects of Spain	MLK, I Have A Dream	9 Things by Jerry Falwell	Reagan Montage
Words per Minute	1427	998	1420	1048	1594	1639	1704
2:00	714	498	708	522	798	822	852
2:10	660	462	654	486	738	756	786
2:20	612	426	606	450	684	702	732
2:30	570	402	570	420	636	654	684
2:40	540	372	534	396	600	612	642
2:50	504	354	504	372	564	576	600
3:00	474	330	474	348	534	546	570
3:10	450	318	450	330	504	516	540
3:20	426	300	426	312	480	492	510
3:30	408	288	408	300	456	468	486
3:40	390	270	390	288	432	450	462
3:50	372	258	372	276	414	426	444
4:00	354	252	354	264	396	408	426
4:10	342	240	342	252	384	396	408
4:20	330	228	330	240	366	378	396
4:30	318	222	318	234	354	366	378
4:40	306	216	306	222	342	354	366
4:50	294	204	294	216	330	342	354
5:00	288	198	282	210	318	330	342

Directions: Skimming Development Graph

Moving on to the Skimming Development Graph, enter your comprehension score in the box directly under the article title. Then, follow the line below the box until it intersects with the WPM that you accomplished/recorded for each article. Place a dot on the axis of the intersection. You may trace your development in the form of a line graph as you move through the readings.

	Show Comp. Scores Here	Bill of Rights	Lincoln's Second Inaugural Address	Churchill, Blood, Sweat, Tears	J. Hart, Why My Voice Matters	Billy Graham, Pastor to Presidents	M. Konrad, Why the Revolution Worked	JFK Inaugural Speech
1000								
975								
950								
925								
900								
875								
850								
825								
800								
775								
750								
725								
700								
675								
650								
625								
600								
575								
550								
525								
500								
475								
450								
425								
400								
375								
350								
325								
300								
275								
250								

	Show Comp. Scores Here	FDR, Fear Itself	D.Sanner, Habits vs. Time	B. Taylor, Christian Missions in Alaska	B.Bell, Aspects of Spain	MLK, I Have A Dream	9 Things by Jerry Falwell	Reagan Montage
1000								
975								
950								
925								
900								
875								
850								
825								
800								
775								
750								
725								
700								
675								
650								
625								
600								
575								
550								
525								
500								
475								
450								
425								
400								
375								
350								
325								
300								
275								
250								

SCANNING

SCANNING INSTRUCTIONS

Scanning involves rapidly covering a great deal of material in order to locate specific information.

I.   Scanning is helpful for locating specific items such as a date, a statistic, or a fact without reading the entire selection.

II. Steps for scanning material:

   A. Always keep in mind the item for which you are searching. If you can hold the image of the word or fact or idea clearly in mind, it is more likely to stand out than surrounding words.

   B. Anticipate the form in which the information is likely to appear—numbers, proper nouns, last name first, etc.

   C. Note the arrangement of the information
      1. Alphabetical
      2. Non-alphabetical: chronological (day/time, month/year), categories, numerical.
      3. Prose: newspapers, magazine articles, encyclopedias, textbooks, nonfiction trade books.

   D. Analyze the organization of the content before you begin to scan.
      1. If the material is familiar or fairly brief, you may be able to scan the entire article/set of information in a single search.
      2. If the material is lengthy or very difficult, a preliminary scan may be necessary and helpful to determine which part of the material is most likely to contain the desired answer.

   E. Let your eyes run rapidly over several lines of print at a time as you search.

   F. When you find the section that has the information you need, make note of the section.

   G. If you are reading an article, read the full sentence which contains the needed information for clarity.

III. In the scanning process, you must be willing to skip over large sections of text without reading or understanding them.

IV. Goal in scanning = 100% accuracy

V.   Scanning can be done at 1,500 Words Per Minute (WPM) or more.

VI. Comparative Ponderings: Compare your reading time and the time spent finding answers as you move through the section.

Scanning: Scanning results will vary with the format of the item that you are scanning. For some students, directories are difficult while others may find schedules or tables more complicated.

VII. In order to produce mastery of various reading formats, exercises and articles will be displayed in a variety of layouts.

ALPHABETICAL LISTING: ANIMALS

Begin the timer and then scan the second part of this exercise for the answers to the following questions. As you find the answers, place them in the blank provided. List the animal name immediately <u>preceding</u> the one noted. Correct spelling is required. When you are finished, immediately stop the timer and note the time in the space provided at the end of the questions. Grade your answers and put the number correct in the space provided below.

Example: lamb, leopard, lion, lionfish

A. Leopard   Answer = lamb

1. Dart frog   1.
2. Bangle Tiger   2.
3. Boar   3.
4. Horn Shark   4.
5. Impala   5.
6. Gazelle   6.
7. Ferret   7.
8. Baboon   8.
9. Hammerhead Shark   9.
10. Dusky Shark   10.
11. Galapagos Shark   11.
12. Hawaiian Monk Seal   12.
13. Bengal Tiger   13.
14. Cougar   14.
15. Chipmunk   15.
16. Giraffe   16.
17. Aardwolf   17.
18. Caribou   18.
19. Jackal   19.
20. Bottlenose Dolphin   20.

```
TIME:
NUMBER CORRECT:
```

ANIMALS LISTING

Aardvark

Aardwolf

African Elephant

African Tree Pangolin

Alligator

Alpaca

Anteater

Antelope

Ape(s)

Arabian Horse

Armadillo

Arthropod(s)

Asian Elephant

Aye-Aye

Baboon

Badger

Bandicoot

Bangle Tiger

Bat(s)

Bearded Dragon

Beaver

Beluga Whale

Bengal Tiger

Big-Horned Sheep

Billy Goat

Bird(s)

Bison

Black Bear

Black Footed Rhino

Black Howler Monkey

Black Rhino

Blacktip Reef Shark

Blue Shark

Blue Whale

Boar

Bob-Cat

Bonobo

Bottlenose Dolphin

Bottlenose Whale

Brown Bear

Buffalo

Bull

Bull frog

Caiman Lizard

Capybara

Camel Capuchin Monkey

Caribou

Cat(s)

Cattle

Cheetah

Chimpanzee

Chinchilla

Chipmunk

Common Dolphin

Common Seal

Coral(s) and Anemone(s)

Cougar

Cow(s)

Coyote

Crocodile

Crustacean(s)

Dart Frog

Deer

Degus Dik-Dik

Dingo

Dog(s)

Dogfish Shark

Dolphin

Donkey

Door Mouse

Dormouse

Draft Horse

Duckbill Platypus

Dugong

Dusky Shark

Elephant

Elephant Seal

Elk

Ermine

Eurasian Lynx

Ferret

Fishes

Florida Panther

Flying Fox

Fox

Fresh Water Crocodile

Frog Fur Seal

Galapagos Land Iguana

Galapagos Shark

Galapagos Tortoise

Gazelle

Gecko

Giant Anteater

Giant Panda

Gibbon

Giraffe

Goat

Gopher

Gorilla

Gray Fox

Gray Nurse Shark

Gray Reef Shark

Gray Whale

Great White Shark

Green Poison Dart Frog

Green Sea Turtle

Grizzly Bear

Groundhog

Guinea Pig

Hairy-Nosed Wombat

Hammerhead Shark

Harbor Porpoise

Harbor Seal

Hare Harp Seal

Hawaiian Monk Seal

Hedgehog

Hippopotamus

Horn Shark

Horse(s)

Howler Monkey

Humpback Whale

Hyena

Hyrax

Iguana

Iguanodon

Impala

Insect(s)

Irrawaddy Dolphin

Jackal

Jackrabbit

Jaguar

Jellyfish

Kangaroo

Kermode Bear

ALPHABETICAL LISTING: DINOSAURS

Begin the timer and then scan the second part of this exercise for the answers to the following questions. As you find the answers, place them in the blank provided. List the dinosaur name immediately following the one noted. Correct spelling is required. When you are finished, immediately stop the timer and note the time in the space provided at the end of the questions. Grade your answers and put the number correct in the space provided below.

Example: ectodon, girodon, hapadon

A. Girodon   Answer = hapadon

1. Bahariasaurus   1.
2. Aardonyx   2.
3. Echinodon   3.
4. Edmontosaurus   4.
5. Centrosaurus   5.
6. Cerasinops   6.
7. Eocursor   7.
8. Anabisetia   8.
9. Amargasaurus   9.
10. Chialingosaurus   10.
11. Animantarx   11.
12. Byronosaurus   12.
13. Agustinia   13.
14. Epachthosaurus   14.
15. Chubutisaurus   15.
16. Brontomerus   16.
17. Drinker   17.
18. Alvarezsaurus   18.
19. Chasmosaurus   19.
20. Camptosaurus   20.

```
TIME:
NUMBER CORRECT:
```

DINOSAURS LISTING

Aardonyx
Abelisaurus
Abrictosaurus
Abrosaurus
Abydosaurus
Acanthopholis
Achelousaurus
Achillobator
Acrocanthosaurus
Adamantisaurus
Adasaurus
Adeopapposaurus
Aegyptosaurus
Aeolosaurus
Aerosteon
Afrovenator
Agilisaurus
Agustinia
Alamosaurus
Alaskacephale
Albertonykus
Albertosaurus
Alectrosaurus
Aletopelta
Alioramus
Allosaurus
Altirhinus
Alvarezsaurus
Alxasaurus
Amargasaurus

Amazonsaurus
Ammosaurus
Ampelosaurus
Amphicoelias
Amurosaurus
Anabisetia
Anatosaurus
Anatotitan
Anchiornis
Anchisaurus
Andesaurus
Angaturama
Angolatitan
Angulomastacator
Animantarx
Bactrosaurus
Bagaceratops
Bagaraatan
Bahariasaurus
Balaur
Bambiraptor
Barapasaurus
Barosaurus
Baryonyx
Becklespinax
Beipiaosaurus
Beishanlong
Bellusaurus
Bistahieversor

Bonitasaura
Borogovia
Bothriospondylus
Brachiosaurus
Brachyceratops
Brachylophosaurus
Brachytrachelopan
Brontomerus
Bruhathkayosaurus
Buitreraptor
Byronosaurus
Camarasaurus
Camelotia
Camptosaurus
Carcharodontosaurus
Carnotaurus
Caudipteryx
Centrosaurus
Cerasinops
Ceratonykus
Ceratosaurus
Cetiosauriscus
Cetiosaurus
Chaoyangsaurus
Charonosaurus
Chasmosaurus
Chialingosaurus
Chilantaisaurus
Chindesaurus

Chirostenotes

Chubutisaurus

Dacentrurus

Daemonosaurus

Daspletosaurus

Datousaurus

Deinocheirus

Deinonychus

Deltadromeus

Diabloceratops

Diamantinasaurus

Diceratops

Dicraeosaurus

Dilong

Dilophosaurus

Dimetrodon

Diplodocus

Dollodon

Dracopelta

Dracorex

Dravidosaurus

Drinker

Dromaeosaurus

Dromiceiomimus

Dryosaurus

Dryptosaurus

Dubreuillosaurus

Dyslocosaurus

Dystrophaeus

Echinodon

Edmarka

Edmontonia

Edmontosaurus

Efraasia

Einiosaurus

Ekrixinatosaurus

Elaphrosaurus

Elrhazosaurus

Enigmosaurus

Eocarcharia

Eocursor

Eodromaeus

Eolambia

Eoraptor

Eotyrannus

Epachthosaurus

Epidendrosaurus

ALPHABETICAL LISTING: ARTISTS

Begin the timer and then scan the second part of this exercise for the answers to the following questions. As you find the answers, place them in the blank provided. List the artist's name immediately <u>preceding</u> the one noted. Correct spelling is required. When you are finished, immediately stop the timer and note the time in the space provided at the end of the questions. Grade your answers and put the number correct in the space provided below.

Example: Cezanne, Picasso, Rembrandt

A.   Rembrandt   Answer = picasso

1.	da Lodi, Giovanni Agostino	1.
2.	Carnevale, Fra	2.
3.	dal Ponte, Giovanni	3.
4.	Bellini, Giovanni	4.
5.	Angelico, Fra	5.
6.	Christus, Petrus	6.
7.	Boccaccino, Boccaccio	7.
8.	de Backer, Jacob	8.
9.	Bermejo, Bartolome	9.
10.	Coornhert, Dirck Volkertszoon	10.
11.	Dalmau, Luis	11.
12.	Bugiardini, Guiliano	12.
13.	Cock, Hieronymus	13.
14.	Alberti, Leon Baptista	14.
15.	da Nola, Giovanni	15.
16.	Crivelli, Carlo	16.
17.	Barbet, Jean	17.
18.	Bregno, Antonio	18.
19.	Blondeel, Lancelot	19.
20.	Daucher, Adolf	20.

```
TIME:
NUMBER CORRECT:
```

ARTISTS LISTING

Aertsen, Pieter

Alberti, Leon Baptista

Albertinelli, Mariotto

Aldegrever, Heinrich

Altdorfer, Albrecht

Amadeo, Giovanni Antonio

Andrea, Zoan

Angelico, Fra

Anselmi, Michelangelo

Antico

Araldi, Alessandro

Aretino, Spinello

Attavanti, Attavante Degli

Bacchiacca, Francesco

Baldovinetti, Alessio

Bambaia

Barbet, Jean

Barendsz, Dirck

Barthel Bruyn the Elder

Bartolommeo, Fra

Basaiti, Marco

Bassano, Jacopo

Bastiani, Lazzaro

Beccaruzzi, Francesco

Beck, LeonhardBeham, Barthel

Beham, Hans Sebald

Bellano, Bartolomeo

Bellegambe, Jean

Bellini, Gentile

Bellini, Giovanni

Bembo, Bonifacio

Benaglio, Francesco

Bening, Simon

Benson, Ambrosius

Bergognone

Bermejo, Bartolome

Bernat, Martin

Berruguete, Pedro

Bertram, Master

Beuckelaer, Joachim

Binck, Jacob

Blondeel, Lancelot

Boccaccino, Boccaccio

Boccaccino, Camillo

Boccati, Giovanni

Bol, Hans

Boltraffio, Giovanni Antonio

Bon, Bartolomeo

Bonfigli, Benedetto

Bonsignori, Francesco

Bordone, Paris

Bosch, Hieronymus

Botticelli, Sandro

Botticini, Francesco

Bouts, Aelbrecht

Bramante, Donato

Bramantino

Bregno, Andrea

Bregno, Antonio

Briosco, Benedetto

Brunelleschi, Filippo

Brusasorci

Bugiardini, Giuliano

Buonarroti, Michelangelo

Butinone, Bernardino Jacopi

Calvaert, Denys

Campagnola, Domenico

Campagnola, Giulio

Campi, Giulio

Campin, Robert

Caporali, Bartolommeo

Capriolo, Domenico

Caraglio, Gian Jacopo

Cariani, Giovanni

Carnevale, Fra

Caroto, Giovanni Francesco

Carpaccio, Vittore

Cazzaniga, Tommaso

Christus, Petrus

Civitale, Matteo

Claeissens I, Pieter

Cock, Hieronymus

Congnet, Gillis

Coornhert, Dirck Volkertszoon

Costa, Lorenzo

Cozzarelli, Giacomo

Cozzarelli, Guidoccio

Crivelli, Carlo

Crivelli, Vittorio

da Besozzo, Michelino

da Brescia, Moretto

da Carpi, Girolamo

da Conegliano, Giambattista Cima

da Fabriano, Antonio

da Fiesole, Mino

da Firenze, Biagio d'Antonio

da Forli, Melozzo

da Lodi, Giovanni Agostino

da Maiano, Benedetto

da Messina, Antonello

da Modena, Giovanni

da Nola, Giovanni

da Panicale, Masolino

da Pavia, Belbello

da Rho, Pietro

da Rimini, Giovanni Francesco

da Rovezzano, Benedetto

da Sangallo, Francesco

da Sangallo, Giuliano

da Sesto, Cesare

da Settignano, Desiderio

da Tolmezzo, Domenicoda

da Udine, Giovanni Martini

da Urbino, Clemente

da Verona, Liberale

da Verona, Michele

da Vinci, Leonardo

Daddi, Bernardo

dal Ponte, Giovanni

Dalmata, Giovanni

Dalmau, Luis

Daret, Jacques

Daucher, Adolf

David, Gerard

de Backer, Jacob

STATE GOVERNMENT DIRECTORY

Begin the timer and then scan the second part of this exercise for the answers to the following questions. As you find the answers, place them in the blank provided. When you are finished, immediately stop the timer and note the time in the space provided at the end of the questions. Grade your answers and put the number correct in the space provided below.

1. On which page would you find the Personnel Division? _____

2. How many headings are under Bar, West Virginia State? _____

3. Which page numbers are not noted in the listing? _____

4. What does FARS stand for? _____

5. This county has the OIG/OHFLAC Division in the Department of Health/Human Resources: _____

6. Listings for which department span pp. 28-30? _____
   _____

7. If you were disabled, which page would you use to seek services? _____

8. Which listing precedes Higher Education? _____

9. How many listings are labeled Divisions? _____

10. How many institutions of higher learning are listed? _____

11. The Ethics Commission follows which listing? _____

12. In which listing does the word "Grievance" appear? _____

13. If you wanted to know about the Office of State Aviation, which page would you turn to? _____

14. If you wanted information on the Arts, on which page would you look? _____

15. On which page(s) would you find both the Accounting Division and the Chief Inspector Division? _____

16. Which page number(s) has/have five listings? _____

17. On page 9, you can find which Center? _____

18. Which word begins the listing after the Westover listing? _____

19. Which county in all caps would come last in an alphabetical listing? _____

20. How many times does the word "Communications" appear in the listings? _____

```
TIME:
NUMBER CORRECT:
```

STATE GOVERNMENT DIRECTORY...PAGE

NOTARY PUBLIC

Begin the timer and then scan the form, in the second part of the exercise for the answers to the following questions. As you find the answers, place them in the blank provided or circle True/False. When you are finished, immediately stop the timer and note the time in the space provided at the end of the questions. Grade your answers and put the number correct in the space provided below.

1. Approved commission must be claimed how many days after issuance?

2. True/False: A notary cannot notarize his own signature.

3. True/False: A notary must charge a fee for his/her services.

4. If a fee is charged, it may not be more than $_____ per document.

5. Updates in the notary handbook are published by what date?

6. True/False: A notary can notarize a birth certificate.

7. If your commission has not been received within four weeks, you would contact the Secretary of the _____.

8. Stamps and seals may be ordered through an _____ vendor.

9. True/False: A notary may notarize a marriage certificate.

10. A notary must be completely satisfied with the _____ of a person whose signature is being notarized.

11. True/False: A notary cannot perform any act that constitutes the practice of law.

12. A notary must always note the date his/her commission will _____.

13. In completing this portion of this form, each section must be _____ to indicate that you understand the information which has been provided.

14. A Virginia _____ must notarize the application before is it submitted.

15. True/False: A notary may choose to include his/her registration number of a document being notarized.

16. The handbook for notaries is titled "The Handbook for Virginia Notaries _____."

17. If incorrect information is given on the application, the applicant is guilty of _____.

18. True/False: Complete notarization must take place on the same page as the signatures being notarized.

19. True/False: A notary may notarize an original, not a copy of, a death certificate.

20. The notary must never accept the word of a _____ party

as being sufficient for identification to justify notarizing a person's signature.

```
TIME:
NUMBER CORRECT:
```

PART 2 AND 3 OF APPLICATION FOR APPOINTMENT AS VIRGINIA NOTARY PUBLIC

Part 2: **Each statement must be initialed indicating that you understand the information provided.**

_____ A Virginia Notary Public must be familiar with and understand everything contained in "The Handbook for VirginiaW Notaries Public" throughout their term as a notary. If changes are made to notary laws, the updated handbook will be available bu July 1. "The Handbook for Virginia Notaries Public" can be found on the website:

www.commonwealth.virginia.gov/OfficialDocuments/Notary/notary.cfm.

_____ A notary must always be completely satisfied with the identity of the person whose signature is being notarized. A notary is not obligated to notarize a peron's signature without being sure that the person is who he or she claims to be. Always check identification and be stisfied that the identification and be satisfied that the identification is alid. Never accept the word of a third party as being sufficient for identification to justify notarizing person's signature.

_____ A notary is not required to charge fee for his or her services, but if a fee is charged, it cannot be more than $5.00 for each document notarized.

_____ A notary *cannot* notarize birth, marriage, death certificates (original or copies) or perform marrigaes.

_____ A notary *cannot* perform any act that constitutes the practice of law.

_____ The notary must notify the Secretary of the Commonwealth's Office of any changes to the information provided on their application during the course of their commission.

_____ There are seven (7) items required for the notary to state on each document being notarized:
   1. The name of the county or independent city in which th document is signed
   2. The date the document is signed
   3. The notarial statement - what is being notarized
   4. The notary's signature
   5. The date that the notary's commission expires
   6. Notary registration number
   7. Photographically reproducible notary seal/stamp

_____ Every effort should be made to have complete notarization on the same page as the signature(s) being notarized. If notarization is on a separate page from signature(s), the notarial statement must include the name of each person whose signature is being notarized.

_____ A Virginia notary's seal must contain the name of the notary exactly as it appears on the notary's commission, words "Notary Public" and "Commonwealth of Virginia." Stamps/seals must be ordered through an outside vendor. The office of the Secretary of the Commonwealth does not sell or make notary stamps/seals.

_____ **By law, you must claim your commission within 60 days after it is issued.** If you fail to do so you must submit a new application and a new fee to become a Notary. If you have not received your ommission within four weeks call the Secretary of the Commonwealth's Office at (804)692-2356 or by email to socmail@governor.virginia.gov. Sometimes notices are lost in the mail. Failure to receive a notice will not permit you to receive a commission after the 60-day period has expired.

Part 3: **MUST be notarized by a Virginia Notary before submitting application**

I,_____, solemnly swar or affirm under penalty of perjury that the information in this application is true, complete and correct; that I understand the official duties and responsibilities of a notary public in the Commonwealth of Virginia, as described in the statutes; and that I will perform to the best of my ability all notrial acts in accordance with the law.

Signature of Applicant: _____
(This signature must match the name on line 1 of this application and must be used in signing ALL notarized documents)

*****TO BE COMPLETED BY VIRGINIA NOTARY BEFORE SUBMITTING *****

Commonwealth of Virginia - City/Council of _____

Sworn and subscribed before me this _____ day of _____, 20_____

Signature of Notary Public: _____

Notary Registration Number:_____

My Commission Expires: _____,20_____

PARKS AND RECREATION

Begin the timer and then scan the form in the second part of the exercise for the answers to the following questions. As you find the answers, place them in the blank provided. Be sure to use number words (one, two, etc.) when a number is the requested answer. When you are finished, immediately stop the timer and note the time in the space provided at the end of the questions. Grade your answers and put the number correct in the space provided below.

1. At which Natural Area can people go fishing and find restrooms? _____

2. How many Community Parks have picnic shelters? _____

3. Which park on Jefferson Street has trails? _____

4. Which park has the most possibilities for activities? _____

5. How many parks have canoe ramps? _____

6. Which Community Park has the most acreage? _____

7. Which park is apparently on a corner? _____

8. Which park has disc golf? _____

9. Speeches, music, etc. must be kept below what distance of amplification? _____

10. In which parks are alcoholic beverages allowed? _____

11. How many Neighborhood Parks have more than 10 acres of land? _____

12. How many Neighborhood Parks have less than five activity possibilities? _____

13. If you wanted to play horseshoes where there is a playground, which Community Park would you visit? _____

14. If you want to let your pet run free with you on a trail, which park would you choose? _____

15. Which type/category of park has the most mountain bike trails? _____

16. At what address would someone find the Neighborhood Park with the most activities? _____

17. Which parks have the smallest acreage? _____

18. and _____

19. Which is the only Neighborhood Park with trails? _____

20. Which park would one visit if they wanted to walk trails, use a grill, and go swimming? _____

TIME:
NUMBER CORRECT:

PARKS & RECREATION INFORMATION

- VIST YOUR PARK ONLY DURING POSTED HOURS

- ALCOHOLIC BEVERAGES AND OTHER CONTROLLED SUBSTANCES ARE PROHIBITED

- MOTORIZED VEHICLES ARE PROHIBITED EXCEPT IN PARKING AREAS AND DESIGNATED ROADWAYS

- NO LITTERING OR GLASS CONTAINERS ALLOWED

- KEEP YOUR PET ON A LEASH

- THE AMPLIFICATION OF MUSIC, SPEECHES, OR ANY OTHER SOUND AUDIBLE BEYOND 25' IS PROHIBITED EXCEPT UPON WRITTEN PERMISSION FROM THE DIRECTOR OF PARKS AND RECREATION

- NO ONE SHALL LEAVE A MOTOR VEHICLE IN CITY PARKS AFTER POSTED HOURS OF OPERATION

- THE COLLECTION, DESTRUCTION AND/OR REMOVAL OF PLANTS, ANIMALS, MINERALS OR HISTORICAL/ CULTURAL ITEMS ARE STRICTLY FORBIDDEN

Parks

	ADDRESSES	ACREAGE	ATHLETIC FIELDS	BASKETBALL	CANOE RAMP	CONCESSIONS	DISC GOLF	FISHING	GRILLS	HORSESHOE COURTS	MTN. BIKE TRAILS	PARKING	PICNIC SHELTER	PICNIC AREA	PLAYGROUND	RESTROOMS	SWIMMING POOL	TENNIS COURTS	TRAILS
COMMUNITY PARKS																			
Blackwater Creek Athletic Area	515 Monticello Avenue	20	*					*	*							*			*
Hollins Mill Park	1711 Hollins Mill Road	3						*	*			*	*	*					*
Ivy Creek Park	225 Jefferson Ridge Parkway	29						*	*	*		*	*	*	*	*			*
James River Canoe Ramp	20 Adams Street				*														
Miller Park	Park Ave. & Fort Avenue	37	*			*			*			*	*	*	*	*	*		*
Peaks View Park	170 Ivy Creek Drive	250	*			*	*		*	*	*	*	*	*	*	*		*	*
Riverfront Park	1000 Jefferson Street	2										*							*
Riverside Park	2238 Rivermont Avenue	47	*						*			*	*	*	*	*		*	*
NATURAL AREA																			
Blackwater Creek Natural Area	515 Monticello Avenue	297	*					*		*		*	*	*		*			*
Percival's Island Natural Area	1600 Concord Turnpike	56						*			*	*	*	*					*
NEIGHBORHOOD PARKS																			
Aubrey Barbour Park	109 Jackson Street	0.5	*																
Biggers Neighborhood Park	501 5th Street	0.5	*						*			*	*		*				
College Park	3200 College Drive	5	*						*				*	*	*				
Fort Ave. Neighborhood Park	4801 Fort Avenue	0.5	*						*				*	*	*				
Heritage Park	531 Leesville Road	59								*		*						*	
Jefferson Park	315 Chambers Street	23	*						*	*		*	*	*	*			*	
Sandusky Park	5805 Rhonda Road	17	*									*	*	*	*				
Valleyview Playlot	1417 4th Street	0.3							*				*	*	*				*
Westover Neighborhood Park	3117 Memorial Avenue	0.3	*						*			*	*	*	*				
Younger Park	2338 Light Street	5	*						*				*	*	*				

FOOTBALL ROSTER

Begin the timer and then scan the form for the answers to the following questions. As you find the answers, place them in the blank provided. When you are finished, immediately stop the timer and note the time in the space provided at the end of the questions. Grade your answers and put the number correct in the space provided below.

1. Which state are the most players from?

2. How many players are from Florida?

3. Who is the quarterback from Clearwater, Florida?

4. How many players weigh over 250 lbs?

5. How many freshmen are from VA?

6. How many players are from the West Coast?

7. How many redshirted freshmen (R) are on the roster?

8. How many players named Brown are from VA?

9. How many wide receivers (WR) are seniors?

10. How many players are 5'10" or taller?

11. Which state has the 2nd highest representation?

12. How many total senior players are on the roster?

13. Which defensive back (DB) is from Sellersville, PA?

14. Who is heavier—the quarterback (QB) from FL or SC?

15. How many players are from VA?

16. Is the wide receiver (WR) from Orlando, FL taller than the one from Lynchburg, VA?

17. Which sophomore is the heaviest?

18. How many redshirted (R) players are on the roster?

19. Where is the kicker (K) from?

20. How many players are from SC?

1. _____

2. _____

3. _____

4. _____

5. _____

6. _____

7. _____

8. _____

9. _____

10. _____

11. _____

12. _____

13. _____

14. _____

15. _____

16. _____

17. _____

18. _____

19. _____

20. _____

TIME:

NUMBER CORRECT:

FOOTBALL ROSTER

41	Terry Adams	DL	R-Sophomore	5-11	235	Elkin, NC
29	Alfonso Bailey	DB	Sophomore	5-9	185	Fort Myers, FL
58	Mamadou Balde	LB	R-Junior	6-1	230	Moon Twp., PA
51	Patrick Bannon	OLB	Sophomore	6-4	230	Lexington, VA
49	Matt Bevins	K/P	Freshman	6-2	185	Newport News, VA
46	Derek Bishop	FB	Junior	5-10	225	Bradenton, FL
87	Mark Blakeney	WR	R-Freshman	6-2	200	Midlothian, VA
9	Dominic Bolden	WR	Senior	5-10	180	Orlando, FL
59	Doncel Bolt	ILB	Sophomore	6-2	245	Long Beach, CA
12	Tyler Brennan	QB	Freshman	6-3	205	Anderson, SC
5	Danny Broggin	WR	R-Sophomore	6-0	190	Brookneal, VA
77	Aaron Brown	OL	R-Freshman	6-4	280	South Hill, VA
95	Chad Brown	ILB	R-Sophomore	6-2	240	Melbourne, FL
10	Mike Brown	QB	R-Freshman	6-0	190	Charlottesville, VA
2	Patrick Calvary	DB	Senior	5-9	180	Bradenton, FL
63	Matt Camire	OL	R-Sophomore	6-3	270	Midlothian, VA
29	Brit Campbell	WR	Freshman	6-1	190	Lynchburg, VA
98	Asa Chapman	DL	Freshman	6-5	377	Orange, VA
35	Wes Cheek	RB	Junior	6-0	205	Dacula, GA
32	Ian Childress	LB	Senior	6-4	225	Bedford, VA
17	Larry Claiborne	DB	R-Freshman	6-1	180	Ringgold, VA
19	Omar Clark	DB	R-Freshman	6-0	185	Ringgold, VA
94	Jay Coady	NG	R-Senior	6-1	275	Forest, VA
11	Mike Connolly	OLB	R-Freshman	6-2	235	Sarasota, FL
60	Mario Cosby	OL	R-Junior	6-1	270	Lynchburg, VA
8	Jonathan Crawford	WR	R-Senior	6-0	215	Staunton, VA
86	Steven Crawford	WR	Freshman	6-2	190	Lehigh Acres, FL
84	Ryan Culkin	TE	R-Sophomore	6-4	225	Indian Rocks Beach, FL
69	Zach Davis	OL	R-Senior	6-4	290	Jacksonville, FL
19	Kyle DeArmon	QB	R-Sophomore	6-3	185	Clearwater, FL
20	Chuck Duffey	DB	R-Junior	6-0	190	Lakeland, FL
90	Colin Dugan	NG	Senior	6-0	290	Springdale, PA
16	Jimmy Eden	WR	Freshman	5-10	175	Peachtree City, GA
43	Jamal Giddens	OLB	Freshman	6-2	210	Norfolk, VA

52	Cameron Gillespie	ILB	R-Junior	5-10	245	Federal Way, WA
55	Mike Godsil	OL	Senior	6-2	290	Mansfield, OH
24	Ryan Greiser	DB	Senior	6-1	205	Sellersville, PA
65	Tim Hartman	OL	R-Junior	6-4	315	Chester, VA
25	B. J. Hayes	RB	R-Freshman	5-9	185	Valentines, VA
79	Stan Herring	DL	Freshman	6-4	275	Woodstock, GA
81	Aaron Hewlett	WR	R-Junior	5-7	165	Virginia Beach, VA
26	Kent Hicks	DB	R-Senior	6-2	200	Culpepper, VA
67	Spencer Hodges	OL	R-Freshman	6-5	300	Bradenton, FL
53	Nick Hursky	LB	Senior	6-1	235	Carnegie, PA
99	Ryan Jackson	DL	Freshman	6-3	280	Forest, VA
92	Trey Jacobs	DL	Junior	6-3	280	Columbia, SC
23	Rashad Jennings	RB	Senior	6-1	230	Forest, VA
85	Dominique Jones	TE	R-Junior	6-1	260	San Diego, CA
18	Matt Lambros	WR	Senior	6-3	210	Calgary, Canada
15	Spencer Landis	QB	Junior	6-2	185	Dacula, GA
47	Mike Larsson	K	Freshman	5-10	170	Monroe, NC
34	Terron Lawrence	RB	R-Junior	5-7	175	Wake Forest, NC
28	Kajuan Lee	DB	R-Freshman	5-11	180	Newport News, VA
36	Julian LiDrazzah	RB	R-Junior	5-8	200	Woodland, WA
45	Derek Lisko	OLB	R-Junior	6-0	225	Flower Mound, TX
78	Andy Lundy	OL	Freshman	6-5	305	Chilhowie, Va.
47	Mark Malvaso	FB	R-Junior	6-0	225	Norwalk, Conn.
31	Donald Manns	DB	Junior	5-10	180	Jacksonville, Fla.
6	Reggie Matthews	DB	Freshman	6-0	190	Fort Lauderdale, Fla.
21	Chris McAlister	DB	R-Freshman	6-1	180	Lynchburg, Va.
56	Bryan Mosier	OL	R-Junior	6-2	300	Mansfield, Ohio
33	Kyle O'Donnell	LB	R-Sophomore	6-2	230	York, Pa.
43	Osita Ofuani	RB	R-Sophomore	5-8	170	Newark, Del.
49	James Pelzer	OLB	Sophomore	6-1	195	Laurel, Md.
98	Rick Personna	DL	R-Junior	6-2	230	Miami, Fla.
42	Dan Pope	LS	R-Senior	6-3	200	Palm City, Fla.
88	Will Quarles	TE	R-Junior	6-2	250	Richmond, Va.
82	Corey Rasberry	TE	R-Senior	6-2	240	Panama City, Fla.
40	Nathan Revell	FB	R-Sophomore	5-10	225	Pompano Beach, Fla.

93	Kevin Richard	DL	R-Senior	6-3	280	Lynchburg, Va.
96	Daryl Robertson	DL	Sophomore	6-3	285	Bedford, Va.
22	Brandon Robinson	DB	Freshman	6-1	175	Waxhaw, N.C.
14	Chris Rocco	DB	Junior	5-10	200	Forest, Va.
4	Eugene Rogers	WR	Senior	6-0	180	Grovetown, Ga.
44	Joey Sandvig	FB	R-Senior	5-10	235	Appomattox, Va.
3	Brandon Saunders	DB	R-Freshman	6-0	185	Laurel, Md.
58	Greg Schuster	DL	Freshman	6-2	275	Waxhaw, N.C.
89	Tommy Shaver	TE	R-Freshman	6-6	250	Hot Springs, Va.
39	Ben Shipps	K	R-Freshman	6-0	130	Venice, Fla.
13	Brock Smith	QB	Senior	6-3	240	Hershey, Pa.
97	Tim Smith	DL	R-Sophomore	6-3	265	High Point, N.C.
62	Alex Stadler	OL	R-Sophomore	6-5	310	Bealeton, Va.
54	Britt Stone	OL	R-Senior	6-2	275	Ozark, Ala.
1	Chris Summers	WR	R-Freshman	6-4	190	Jacksonville, Fla.
70	Antonio Tassara	OL	R-Sophomore	6-8	320	Naples, Fla.
83	Stetson Tchividjian	WR	R-Junior	5-11	185	Fort Lauderdale, Fla.
7	Zach Terrell	RB	Senior	6-0	200	Manassas Park, Va.
48	Pierre Tinsley	ILB	R-Sophomore	6-0	235	Lynchburg, Va.
27	Tim Torrence	DB	Junior	5-8	165	Miramar, Fla.
76	Justin Vargas	OL	R-Sophomore	6-5	285	Jacksonville, Fla.
74	Josh Weaver	OL	R-Junior	6-4	285	Starke, Fla.
30	Alfonso Wells	RB	R-Sophomore	5-8	175	Woodbridge, Va.
91	Soeren Wendland	DL	R-Sophomore	6-8	300	Cuxhaven, Germany
75	Toney White	OL	R-Freshman	6-4	285	Manassas Park, Va.
60	Steven Wilkes	TE	Freshman	6-6	240	Clifton Forge, Va.
37	Terry Williams	RB	R-Sophomore	5-9	185	Miami, Fla.
30	Mannie Willis	DB	R-Junior	5-10	200	Newport News, Va.
61	Matthias Wrede	OL	Junior	6-5	265	Langenhagen, Germany
40	Paul Young	K	Sophomore	6-2	180	Woodbridge, Va.

Head Football Coach: Danny Rocco (Wake Forest ('84))

Associate Head Coach/Tight Ends: Pete Sundheim (Delaware ('71))

Assistant Head Coach/Off. Coordinator/Off. Line: Scott Wachenheim (Air Force Academy ('84))

Defensive Coordinator: Tom Clark (Maryland ('86))

Assistant Coach - Running Backs: Frank Hickson (Tuskegee ('83))

Assistant Coach - Defensive Backs: Marshall Roberts (Rutgers ('93))

Assistant Coach - Wide Receivers/Recruiting Coor.: Charlie Skalaski (Florida ('78))

Passing Game Coordinator/Quarterbacks: Brandon Streeter (Clemson ('99))

Assistant Coach - Defensive Line/Special Teams: Chad Wilt (Taylor ('00))

Director of High School Relations/Linebackers: Robert Wimberly (Alabama A&M ('02))

Assistant Athletics Director For Football Administ: Paul Rutigliano

Director of Spiritual Development: Ed Gomes (Liberty ('76))

Head Equipment Manager: Mike Morris

Assistant Equipment Manager: Chris Brown (Liberty ('07))

Video Coordinator: Danny Wenger (Liberty, ('97))

Academic Coordinator - Football: Andy Coleman

Assistant Athletics Director for Sports Medicine: Chris Casola (Liberty ('91))

Senior Assistant Athletic Trainer - Football: Barry Finke

Head Strength and Conditioning Coordinator: Bill Gillespie (Liberty, ('83))

Associate Strength and Conditioning Coordinator: Dave Williams (Alabama, ('73))

Assistant Director of Operations and Recruiting: Adam Godwin (Liberty ('05))

Administrative Assistant: Bev Cole

AQUATICS: SWIM LESSON CHART

Begin the timer and then scan the second part of the exercise for the answers to the following questions. As you find the answers, place them in the blank provided. When you are finished, immediately stop the timer and note the time in the space provided at the end of the questions. Grade your answers and put the number correct in the space provided below.

1. Earliest time slot for Level 2 Advanced classes? _____

2. Where classes are held? _____

3. General fee charged? _____

4. Dates for only class for adults? _____

5. Length of classes? _____

6. Date for Level 2: Shallow Water class? _____

7. Class number of Pre-School: Level 2, 4-5 yrs.? _____

8. Time for Parent & Child class? _____

9. Must register by what day of the week before a class begins? _____

10. Certifying/sponsoring national organization? _____

11. Earliest date of Level 2: Advanced class? _____

12. Ages allowed in Adult classes? _____

13. Classes meet on which days? _____

14. Number of times classes meet? _____

15. Time of evening classes for Shallow Water class? _____

16. Days reserved for make-up sessions? _____

17. Ages for children in Parent & Child classes? _____

18. Only dates for Combined Pre-School 3 & Level 2? _____

19. Lynchburg resident fee? _____

20. Class # of the only Advanced class for 7-15 yrs.? _____

```
TIME:
NUMBER CORRECT:
```

SWIM LESSONS

Choose the American Red Cross Swim Lesson that suits your needs. Individual classes are between 30 and 45 minutes in length. Each class meets a total of eight sessions, Monday through Thursdays. Fridays are reserved for make-up days. All classes are held at the Miller Park Pool. Register by Wednesday before. **Fee $55.00 / LR $40.00**

SWIM LESSONS	AGES	CLASS NUMBER	DATES M-TH	TIMES
PARENT & CHILD	18 months - 3 years	34018.201	6/17-6/27	6:30-7:00pm
	18 months - 3 years	34018.202	7/8-7/18	6:30-7:00pm
PRE-SCHOOL: LEVEL 1	3-4 years	34010.201	6/17-6/27	10:50-11:20am
	3-5 years	34010.202	7/8-7/18	10:10-10:40am
PRE-SCHOOL: LEVEL 2	3-4 years	34010.203	6/17-6/27	10:10-10:40am
	4-5 years	34010.204	6/17-6/27	7:05-7:35pm
	3-4 years	34010.205	7/8-7/18	10:50-11:20am
	4-5 years	34010.206	7/8-7/18	10:50-11:20am
	3-5 years	34010.207	7/29-8/8	10:50-11:20am
LEVEL 2: SHALLOW WATER	4-7 years	34012.201	7/8-7/18	9:20-10:00am
	4-7 years	34012.202	7/8-7/18	7:05-7:45pm
PRE-SCHOOL 3 & LEVEL 2	4-7 years	34012.203	7/29-8/8	10:00-10:40am
LEVEL 2	5-15 years	34012.204	6/17-6/27	9:40-10:25am
	6-15 years	34012.205	6/17-6/27	6:30-7:15pm
	8-15 years	34012.206	7/29-8/8	10:35-11:20am
LEVEL 2: ADVANCED	6-15 years	34012.207	6/17-6/27	10:35-11:20am
	6-15 years	34012.208	7/8-7/18	9:55-10:40am
LEVEL 3	6-15 years	34013.201	6/17-6/27	10:35-11:20am
	7-15 years	34013.202	7/8-7/18	6:30-7:15pm
LEVEL 3: ADVANCED	7-15 years	34013.203	7/8-7/18	9:00-9:45am
LEVEL 4	7-15 years	34014.201	6/17-6/27	9:40-10:25am
	8-15 years	34014.202	7/29-8/8	10:35-11:20am
ADULTS	16 years & up	34017.201	7/8-7/18	6:30-7:15pm

PHYSICIANS REGISTRY QUESTIONS

Begin the timer and then scan the second part of the exercise for the answers to the following questions. As you find the answers, place them in the blank provided. When you are finished, immediately stop the timer and note the time in the space provided at the end of the questions. Grade your answers and put the number correct in the space provided below.

1. Who is the lead physician in the Rustburg Family Practice?

    1. _____

2. Who is the Front Office Coordinator at Blue Ridge Immediate Care?

    2. _____

3. What group would I likely call for an advanced ear infection?

    3. _____

4. Who is the Nurse Practitioner at Staunton River Family Physicians?

    4. _____

5. Who is president of The Cardiovascular Group of the Centra Stroobants Heart Center?

    5. _____

6. What is the website for researching gastroenterology?   6. _____

7. What is the number of hospitalists at Medical Associates of Central Virginia, Inc.?

    7. _____

8. Who is the CEO of the Johnson Health Center?   8. _____

9. Who is noted as a pediatric cardiologist?   9. _____

10. Who is the Nurse Practitioner at the Alan B. Pearson Regional Cancer Center?

    10. _____

11. Who is the administrator of Blue Ridge Ear, Nose, Throat, & Plastic Surgery?

    11. _____

12. What is the street address for Monelison Family Physicians?

    12. _____

13. What is the telephone number for the family practice in Rustburg?

    13. _____

14. What is the website for immediate
    care in Blue Ridge?   14. _____

15. Who is the only female physician in
    Forest Family Physicians?   15. _____

16. Where would I find information on
    oncology treatments?   16. _____

17. What doctor is an infection disease specialist?   17. _____

18. What practice appears to have a
    husband/wife practicing?   18. _____

19. Who is noted as a pediatric endocrinologist?   19. _____

20. Who is a family physician in Hurt, VA?   20. _____

```
TIME:
NUMBER CORRECT:
```

PHYSICIANS LIST

PHYSICIANS - *Cardiology*

The Cardiovascular Group of the Centra Stroobants Heart Center
(434) 200-5252
2140 Atherholt Road
Lynchburg, VA 24501
www.thecardiovasculargroup.org
Dr. Justin Anderson
Dr. William Brown
Dr. Daniel Carey
Dr. Fadi El-Ahdab
Dr. Jason Hackenbracht
Dr. Chad Hoyt
Dr. Christopher Meyer
Dr. Thomas Meyer
Dr. Carl Moore
Dr. Ronald Morford
Dr. Thomas Nygaard
Dr. Peter O'Brien
Dr. Matthew Sackett
Dr. Brian Schietinger
Dr. Mark Townsend, Pediatric Cardiologist
Dr. David Truitte
Dr. C. Michael Valentine, President
Dr. William VanDyke

PHYSICIANS - *Ear, Nose & Throat*

Blue Ridge Ear, Nose, Throat & Plastic Surgery
(434) 947-3993
2321 Atherholt Road
Lynchburg, VA 24501
www.BlueRidgeENTPS.com
Dr. Timothy Courville, M.D.
Dr. Graham Gilmer, M.D
Dr. James Hengerer, M.D.
Dr. Joseph Hutchinson, M.D.
Ms. Mary Sue Ramey, Administrator

PHYSICIANS - *Endocrinology*

Endocrinology Associates of Central Virginia
(434) 947-3944
2215 Landover Place
Lynchburg, VA 24501
www.centralvamd.com
Dr. Alan Kauppi, Endocrinologist
Dr. Patricia Powers, Pediatric Endocrinologist
Dr. Lisa Wisniewski, Endocrinologist

PHYSICIANS - *Family Practice*

Central Virginia Family Physicians, Inc.
For more information see our ad on page 80
(434) 382-1125
1111 Corporate Park Drive Suite D
Lynchburg, VA 24501
www.cvfp.net

Additional Locations:
Immediate Care
(434) 239-0132
14005 Wards Road, Suite A
Lynchburg, VA
www.cvfp.net
Dr. Keith Metzler
Dr. Christopher VonElten

Amelon Immediate Care
(434) 929-1095
200 Amelon Square
Madison Heights, VA 24572
www.cvfp.net
Dr. Keith Metzler
Dr. Christopher VonElten

Appomattox Family Practice
(434) 352-8235
131 Jones Street
Appomattox, VA 24522
www.cvfp.net
Dr. Verna Guanzon, Physician
Dr. John Hoffman, M.D.
Dr. Ronna Wright, M.D.

Blue Ridge Immediate Care
(434) 845-4175
2137 Lakeside Drive, Suite 100
Lynchburg, VA 24501
www.cvfp.net
Dr. Henry Burgess, Physician
Dr. Paul Foster, Physician
Mr. Mitchell Hodge, Front Office Coordinator
Dr. Christopher VonElten, Physician

Forest Family Physicians
(434) 525-6964
1175 Corporate Park Drive
Forest, VA 24501
www.cvfp.net
Dr. John Carmack, M.D.
Dr. Jarrett Dodd, M.D.
Dr. Thomas Eppes, M.D.
Dr. Leah Hinkle, M.D.
Dr. Mark Kleiner, M.D.

Monelison Family Physicians
(434) 846-8421
4262 South Amherst Highway
Madison Heights, VA 24572
www.cvfp.net
Dr. Richard Bendall, Physician
Dr. Frank Garcia, Physician
Dr. David Haga, Physician

New London Family Practice
(434) 534-6868
1088 London Links Road
Forest, VA 24551
www.cvfp.net
Dr. Laura Robert, Physician
Dr. Richard Stowers, Physician

Pied mont Family Practice
(434) 846 7374
2019 Tate Springs Road
Lynchburg, VA 24501
www.cvfp.net
Dr. Kimberly Combs, Physician
Dr. Michael Okin, Physician
Dr. John Williams, Physician
Dr. David Wodicka, Physician

Rustburg Family Practice
(434) 332-7367
925 Village Highway
Rustburg, VA 24588
www.cvfp.net
Dr. Trudy Shahady, Physician

Staunton River Family Physicians
(434) 324-9150
527 Pocket Road
Hurt, VA 24563
www.cvfp.net
Dr. Robert Elliot, Physician
Ms. Kathy Worley, Nurse Practitioner

Timberlake Family Practice
(434) 237-6471
20304 Timberlake Road
Lynchburg, VA 24502
www.cvfp.net
Dr. Michael Caulkins, Physician
Dr. Pamela Caulkins, Physician
Dr. Louis Graham, Physician
Dr. James VandeWater, Physician

Johnson Health Center
(434) 947-5967
320 Federal Street
Lynchburg, VA 24504
www.jhcvirginia.org
Ms. Carolyn Bagley, CEO

PHYSICIANS - *Gastroenterology*

Gastroenterology Associates of Central Virginia, Inc.
(434) 384-1862
121 Nationwide Drive Suite A
Lynchburg, VA 24502
www.gastrocentralva.com
Dr. Charles Catalano
Dr. Chal Nunn
Dr. Robert Headley
Dr. Robert Richards
Dr. Ralph Wisniewiski

PHYSICIANS - *Hematology & Oncology*

Alan B. Pearson Regional
Cancer Center
(434) 200-5925
Lynchburg Hematology - Oncology
Clinic, Inc
1701 Thomson Drive, Suite 200
Lynchburg, VA 24501
www.cancer.centralhealth.com
  Ms. Phyllis Everett, Nurse Practitioner
  Dr. John Halpin
  Dr. Robert Headley
  Dr. Cecilia MacCallum
  Dr. John MacNeil
  Dr. Dwight Oldham
  Dr. Kathleen Paul

Mr. Joe Guidi, DO, Hospitalist
Dr. Joel Hodges, Hospitalist
Dr. Gabrielle Jackson, Hospitalist
Traci Ogbu, Hospitalist
Dr. James Pittard, Hospitalist
Dr. Wesley Robertson, Hospitalist
Dr. Kaneez Salbia, Hospitalist
Ms. Julie Suppa, MD, Hospitalist
Dr. W. Kirkham Sydnor, III, Hospitalist
Khiem Tran, MD, Hospitalist
Dr. Nathan Williams, Hospitalist
Ms. Laura Yount, MD, Hospitalist

PHYSICIANS - *Internal Medicine*

Internal Medicine Associates
of Central Virginia
(434) 947-3944
2215 Landover Place
Lynchburg, VA 24501
www.centralvamd.com
  Dr. Juan Aponte
  Dr. Robert Brennan
  Dr. Johanna Brown,
    Infectious Diseases Physician
  Dr. David Cannon
  Dr. Daniel Horton
  Dr. Danielle Lewis
  Mr. Archibald Lord, MD
  Dr. Jack Lu
  Dr. Jay Meadows
  Dr. Moira Rafferty
  Dr. Geeta Rakheram
  Dr. J. Scott Wade
  Dr. Christopher Webb
  Dr. Michael Will
  Dr. Eugene Wolanski

Medical Associates of
Central Virginia, Inc.
(434) 947-3944
2215 Landover Place
Lynchburg, VA 24501
www.centralvamd.com
  Dr. Robert Armock, Hospitalist
  Mr. Paul Bennett, MD, Hospitalist
  Dr. Robert Brennan, Hospitalist
  Dr. William Cheatwood, Hospitalist
  Dr. Louis Chi, Hospitalist
  Dr. Charles Coggin, III, Hospitalist
  Dr. Elizabeth Cook, Hospitalist
  Dr. Michael Cook, Hospitalist
  Dr. Tony Farmer, Hospitalist
  Dr. Murat Gezen, Hospitalist

TELEPHONE DIRECTORY

Begin the timer and then scan the second part of the exercise for the answers to the following questions. As you find the answers, place them in the blank provided. When you are finished, immediately stop the timer and note the time in the space provided at the end of the questions. Grade your answers and put the number correct in the space provided below.

1. What is the address for TRBC (Thomas Road Baptist Church)?

   _____

2. What is the 800 number for Investment Services within SunTrust?

   _____

3. If I lived in Moneta, VA and wanted to contact StellarOne Bank, what number would I call?

   _____

4. If I spoke Chinese and had a question about my residential Verizon phone, what number would I call?

   _____

5. If I were looking for a land surveying/engineering company, which business would I call?

   _____

6. If I used SunTrust for my existing mortgage, what number would I call for assistance?

   _____

7. If I lived at Smith Mountain Lake and needed a chiropractor, what address would I use?

   _____

8. If I used Shaklee Products and was looking for a distributor in the medical field, who would I contact?

   _____

9. What doctor would I contact for oral surgery in the Roanoke Valley?

   _____

10. Note the number to contact if my business needed repair service from Verizon.

   _____

11. If I lived in Staunton in the Shenandoah Valley and wanted to go on a tour, what number would I call?

   _____

12. If I needed a number for the U.S. government on Main St., Bedford, which number would I call?

   _____

13. If my profession is farming and I needed my tractor repaired, where would I find a repair shop?

   _____

14. If my dentist is Dr. E. Smith and I needed to call him at home, which number would I call?

   _____

15. How could I connect with the Bank of Fincastle's online services?

   _____

16. If I were a Spanish-speaking homeowner and needed to make payment arrangements with Verizon, which number would I call?

   _____

17. If I were trying to find a professional corporation of doctors specializing in urology, which address would I use?

   _____

18. What funeral home would I find on N. Bridge Street in Bedford?

   _____

19. If I were looking for Mr. Cooper with State Farm Insurance, where would I locate his office?

   _____

20. If I am hearing impaired and deal with SunTrust Banks, what number would I call for assistance?

   _____

```
TIME:
NUMBER CORRECT:
```

TELEPHONE DIRECTORY
S Sco-Ver 6

Scott & Bond INC
Ofc 435 E Main St. Bedford............................ 586-3131
Residence – Nights Sunday & Holiday Call Insurance
Bond Charles B 586-6402
Real Estate
Rush Judy K 871-3131
Rush Steve 871-4021
O'Connor-Wuergler Becky 871-0858
Bond Hugh H 871-0094
Drake StevE 400-5212
Johnson Mark... 874-4655
Claytor Tony 33-9219
Scott & Bond Inc..................................... 586-3132
Scott Pump Sales & Service 297-6589
Scott & Stringfellow 1 Cedar Hill Court........... 586-4422
Scott & Stringfellow Inc
  1 Cedar Hill Ct Bedford 587-7080
Scott's Automotive 1613 Longwood Ext Bedford586-1773
Sears Roebuck and Co Product Repair
Services Window Replacement.................. 800-882-5351
Retail Stores River Ridge
Mall Lynchburg Auto Center 434-582-5295
4812 Valley View Blvd Roanoke
  General Information................................ 563-3838
Sellari Enterprises Inc 106 N Bridge St Bedford586-6767
Sentry Exteriors Bedford VA 890-9185
Sentry Exteriors
  21835 Timberlake Rd Lynchburg....... 434-239-6722
ServPro of Lynchburg Bedford......................... 586-1579
ServPro of Lynchburg
  2583 Stone Mountain Rd Bedford............. 586-1578
Seven Hills Lock & Key Bedford....................... 586-8906
Shaheen & Shaheen PC
  1123 Celebration Av Moneta 297-8904
Shaklee Authorized Distributor
  2727 Melrose Av NW Roanoke................. 344-8753
Shaklee Distributor – Cheryl Z Saville RN,
CNC RN CNC 810 Blue Ridge Av Bedford 586-7374
Shalet Suzanne 1922 Parker Rd Bedford 587-4120
Shear Impressions 11892 Moneta Rd Moneta.. 297-5090
Shelor Chevrolet Toyota Scion Chrysler Dodge Subaru
Ford Kia I-81 Exit 118C Christiansburg 866-743-5671
Shelor Chevrolet Toyota Scion Chrysler Dodge Subaru
Ford Kia 2260 Roanoke St NE Christiansburg . 382-2981
Shelor Chevrolet Toyota Scion Chrysler Dodge Subaru
Ford Kia
  2325 Roanoke St SE Christiansburg ... 866-743-5671
Shelton Steven L ins agnt
  2225 N Augusta St Stanton 800-572-3303
Shenandoah Tours, Inc.
  225 N St Stanton 800-572-3303
Sherman Frank L DDS
  308 E Main St Bedford............................ 586-8080
Sherman's Boat Services
  2612 Tolers Ferry Rd Hudlstn.................. 297-7223
Shoen Daren Ally 202 E Main St Bedford 586-5003
Shoppe The 14559 Moneta Rd Moneta 297-8400
Shrader Engineering & Land Surveying Inc
  119 S Bridge St Bedford........................... 586-4710
Silbro Inc 1142 La Casa Ct Moneta.................. 297-6600
Simmons Insurance Agency
  1170 Celebration Av Moneta 297-2886
Simmons Richard Drilling Co Inc
  60 Drill Rig Dr Buchnn........................... 254-2289
Sines John 214 Bridge St. Bedford.................... 587-6700
Sitzler Emily Rowe PLC
  108 E Main St. Bedford............................ 586-3000
608 Mini Storage Smith Mountain Lake........... 297-3529
Sky Dynamics Corp
1900 Skyway Dr Moneta 297-6754
Skymark Discount Tobacco & More
1087 Moneta Road Bedford 587-3633

Slusher Surveying Associates PC
  107d Turnpike Rd Bedford............................ 586-9157
Smile Broadcasting Llc
  1126 Hendricks Store Rd Moneta.................... 297-7880
Smith C Frederick dnlst
  46 Shelor Dr Lynchburg.................... 434-237-6328
Smith Eric J DDS Residence 297-1597
  Nights Sundays & Holidays Call..................... 297-7737
Smith Eric J Dr 4860 Rucker Rd Moneta 297-7737
Smith Flooring Company 297-2242
Smith George L & Kathryn Hudlstn 297-7753
Smith Mountain Flowers Llc
  14477 Moneta Rd Moneta......................... 297-6524
Smith Mountain Fraternal Order
Of The Eagles Moneta 297-3934
Smith Mountain Lake Airport
  1090 Cullass Rd Moneta........................... 297-4500
Smith Mountain Lake Animal Hospital
  15029 Moneta Rd Moneta......................... 297-9188
Smith Mountain Lake Boat Yard
  16700 Moneta Rd Moneta......................... 297-7070
Smith Mountain Lake Chiropractic Center
  15388 Moneta Rd Moneta......................... 297-1085
Smith Mountain Lake Democrats
  16483 Moneta Rd Moneta......................... 296-0809
Smith Mountain Lake Magic and Science
  1123 Celebration Av Moneta 297-1220
Smith Mountain Lake Moose Lodge No246
  1174 Morgans Church Rd Moneta........... 297-7183
Smith Mountain Lake Reality LLC
  16700 Moneta Rd Moneta......................... 297-6060
Smith Mountain Lake Seventh Day Adventist Church
  10802 Moneta Rd Moneta......................... 296-2225
Smith Mountain Lake State Park Boat Rental
Hudlstn.. 297-3642
Smith Mountain Lake Tree Experts Moneta.... 297-8899
Smith Mountain Lake Landscapes Ltd
  400 Surrey Dr Hudlstn............................ 297-7753
Smith Mountain Trading Post Store
  1022 Trading Post Rd Hudlstn................. 297-2626
Smith Mountain Yacht Club Inc
  1617 Crystal Shores Dr Moneta............... 297-4484
Smokehouse Restaurant
  1123 Celebration Av Moneta 297-4646
Smooth Electric Co
  1100 Dogwood Hills Dr Goode................ 587-5545
Smyth Companies 311 W Depot St Bedford.... 586-2311
Snow's Auto Repair 5208 Forest d Bedford...... 586-4071
Social Security Administration 7168 Timberlake
  Rd Lynchburg Toll Free 800-772-0778
Social Security Administration
  7168 Timberlake Rd Lynchburg......... 800-772-1213
Solstas Network 1613 Oakwood St Bedford..... 586-0558
Southeastern Siloco of VA Inc
  530 Squaw Aly Petrsbrg 804-732-2836
Southern Flavoring Co Inc
  1330 Norfolk Ave Bedford......................... 586-8565
Southern Insurance Company
  of Virginia 800-468-1127
Southern Insurance Company
  of Virginia 800-888-6405
Southern States Bedford Cooperative
  1053 Independence Blvd bedford 586-8201
Southern Stone
  12004 Leesville Rd Lynch Statn............... 297-0012
Speedy Mart 510 Blue Ridge Av Bedford......... 586-8201
Sportsman Restaurant 16111 Smith Mountain
  Lake Pkwy Hudlstn................................ 297-7900
Spring Lake Stock Yard
  1069 Sickle Ct Moneta............................ 297-1707
Stafford Leonard Res
  1767 Rock Cliff Rd Bedford..................... 297-1041
Ofc Rt 3 Bedford....................................... 297-1287
Stanley Jim 586-4141

Stanley Steemer Carpet Cleaner Bedford......... 586-5558
Star City Communications Inc
   513 Blue Ridge Av Bedford....................... 587-0321
State Farm Insurance
   738 Burks Hill Rd Bedford....................... 586-0811
State Farm Insurance Companies Jeff Persinger
   738 Burks Hill Rd Bedford....................... 586-0811
State Farm Mutual Automobile Ins Co Ofc
   116 S Bridge St... 586-8210
State Farm Mutual George N Cooper Jr
   116 S bridge St Bedford 586-8194
State Police Dept Of Toll Free-Dial
   1 & Then 800-542-5959
Staunton Baptist Church 15267 Smith Mountain
Lake Pkwy Hudlstn 297-6753
Staunton River High School............................ 297-2838
Staunton River High School
   1 Golden Eagle Dr Moneta....................... 297-7151
Staunton River Veterinary Clinic
   1037 Lipscomb Rd Moneta....................... 297-1000
StellarOne 125 W Main St Bedford 586-2590
StellarOne 125 W Main St Bedford 586-6026
StellarOne 14739 Moneta Rd Moneta............ 297-1233
StellarOne 14739 Moneta Rd Moneta............ 297-9840
StellarOne Bank
Bedford
   125 W Main St 586-2590
Forest
   14915 Forest Rd Forest 434-525-2000
   125 W Main St Bedford 587-3188
Moneta
   14739 Moneta Rd 297-1233
Steve Saunders Pump Service Moneta 297-7630
Stevens Pluming and Heating & Air Conditioning
1144 Murray Av 345-6496
Stevens Plumbing Heating & Air Conditioning
   1144 Murray Av Roanoke 345-6496
Stevens Russell M 1251 Dickerson Mill Rd 586-3760
Steve's Tree Service
   1416 Old Firetrail Rd Hudlstn 297-3796
Stone Mountain Ltd
   1597 Eagle Point Rd Hudlstn 297-6434
Stop In Food Stores 1602 Forest Rd Bedford .. 586-4941
Stop In Food Stores
   1602 Longwood Av Bedford 586-8927
Stop In Food Stores
   856 Burks Hill Rd Bedford........................ 586-2874
Straightline Performance LLC
   3674 Headens Bridge Rd Bedford 297-0027
Strawberry Baptist Association
   163 W Main St Bedford 586-8345
Street Transmissions
   1459 Mob Creek Rd Bedford 587-0488
Strong Arm Towing And Recovery
   3097 Falling Creek Rd Bedford 707-1964
Strong Arm Towing And Recovery
   3097 Falling Creek Rd Bedford 586-1990
Subway Bedford 586-7227
Subway 1126 E Lynchburg Salem
Trnpk Bedford 586-2845
Suck Spring Baptist Church
   3887 Jopling Road Bedford 586-3709
Sudden Link 888-501-4149
Suggs Appraisal Service
   6728 White House Road Moneta.............. 297-1824
Sun & Style 1088 Moneta Rd Bedford 586-1908
Sunrise Builders 297-7831
Sunshine Entertainment
   2 8345 Moneta Rd Bedford 297-3900
SunTrust
For Customer Service 800-786-8787
TDD Hearing Impaired 800-854-8965
SunTrust Directory Assistance 800-786-8787
Business Services-Loans

Commercial 434-847-2237
Business Banking 434-847-2237
Investment Services 982-3098
Or Call 800-526-1177
Private Wealth Management 434-847-2318
Or Call 800-526-1177
Continued – See next column
Continued – From previous column
SunTrust
Branch and ATM Locations and Hours ... 800-786-8787
Branch Locations
Bedford Office
115 W Main St Bedford 586-0970
SunTrust Bank 115 W Main St Bedford 586-0970
SunTrust Mortgage Inc
Existing Mortgage Inquiries 800-634-7928
SunTrust Mortgage Inc 115 W Main St 586-2742
Super8 842 Sword Beach Ln Bedford 587-0100
Supermedia
The official publisher of Verizon print directories
Client Care .... 866-91 SUPER (78737)
Sales Office 800-875-6190
To Order Directories 800-888-8448
Superpages.com 800-428-8722
Toll Free
SuperMedia LLC .... 866 – 917 – 8737
Surgical Tools Inc Bedford 587-7193
Sweetwater RV Park
4474 White House Rd Moneta 296-0522
Synergy Resource Inc
   3678 Moneta Rd Bedford 586-6160

T

Taco Bell 10010 Independence Blvd Bedford . 586-1199
Tammy's Hair Fashion
   11432 Big Island Hwy Big Island 434-299-5184
Tan Yur Can 1087 Moneta Rd Bedford 587-8859
TANTastic 1123 Celebration Av Moneta 297-8267
Tate Engineering Systems Inc
   2037 Electric Rd Roanoke 265-7733
Tatum Ginny E DVM
1037 Lipscomb Rd Moneta 297-1000
Taylor Brothers
   1052 Independence Blvd Bedford 586-1297
Taylor Insurance Agencies
   806 E Main St Bedford 586-9717
Taylor's New & Used Furniture
   6190 Forest Rd 586-3773
Terminix International 31 Wells St Salem 586-4645
Terry Robert
   8924 Dickerson Mill Rd Moneta 297-7541
Tharp Funeral Home And Crematory
   320 N Bridge St Bedford 586-3443
Tharp Funeral Home & Crematory Inc
   320 N Bridge St Bedford 586-3443
Thaxton Baptist Church Thxtn 586-8348
Thaxton Market
   1010 Little Apple Dr Thaxtn 586-0171
The Agape Center-Ministry of RBC
   12361 N Old Moneta Rd Moneta 296-0609
The Bank of Fincastle
   1387 American Way Ct Bedford 587-6544
The Bank of Fincastle
www.bankoffincastle.com
1387 American Way Ct Bedford 587-6546
The Bedford Area Education Foundation
   325 Washington St Bedford 587-8744
The Bedford Realty 108 E Main St Bedford ... 586-9595
The Computer Repair Shop
   9330 E Lynchburg Salem Trnpk Goode .. 587-9200
The Family Care Center
   12361 N Old Moneta Rd Moneta 296-0609
The Harbour At Hales Ford
   1336 Campers Paradise Tr Moneta 297-9000
The Life Church 217 W Depot St Bedford 586-5470

The Matrixx Group
  1660 Venture Blvd Bedford 586-2871
The Paw Wash Inc 136 W Main St Bedford ... 587-9090
The Pointe Condo Poa
  1217 Graves Harbor Tr Hudlstn 296-1312
The Shepherds Table
  217 W Washington St Bedford 587-6820
The Spa Tech Bedford 586-6196
The Sportsman Marina 16111 Smith
  Mountain Lake Pkwy Hudlstn 297-2020
The Well LLC 1764 Patriot Ln Bedford 587-9000
Thomas Road Baptist Church
  1 Mountain View Rd Lynchburg 434-239-9281
Tilley's Rainbow Vacuum
  2583 Stone Mountain Rd Bedford 297-8215
Timber Ridge Baptist Church
  3234 Timber Ridge Bedford 586-9267
Tinsley Landscaping Service
  229 Leatherwood Pl 875-6151
Tobacco Company No 3
  The Bedford Shopping Plaza Bedford 587-0227
Tommy's Carpet Cleaning Bedford 586-0612
Tom's Barber Shop 800 Blue Ridge Bedford ... 586-1167
Toms Heating & Air
  1303 Angus Hill Lane Bedford 586-8667
Tony's Pizza Bedford 586-4954
Tony's Red Baron Pizza Service Bedford 586-6970
Touch of Class Beauty Salons
  224 Depot St Bedford 586-3343
Town Center Eye Care LLC
  1503 Enterprise Dr Lynchburg 434-832-0711
Town Center Eye Care LLC
  1503 Enterprise Dr Lynchburg 434-832-0736
Tractor Supply Co 1433 E Main St Bedford ... 587-6600
Travelers Insurance Cox Cundiff Insurance Agency
  205 E Cleveland Av Vinton 342-2082
Trend Setters 1766 Patriot Ln Bedford 586-1325
Trevillian Auction Company Inc
  703 Industrial Av Bedford 586-5007
Trident Seafoods Corp
  940 Orange St Bedford 586-1580
Trident Seafoods Corp
  940 Orange St Bedford 707-0112
Trident Seafoods Corp
  940 Orange St Bedford 707-0113
Trinity Baptist Church 586-8010
Triple R 1104 Keeping Way Dr Bedford 586-6152
Trish's Hair Care
  1107 Coolbrook Rd Bedford 586-4287
Trista's Kountry Kitchen LLC
  1117 Moneta Bedford 586-1313
Trivium Estate Llc 7821 Bellevue Rd Forest 586-2823
Tuck Chiropractic Clinic
  1 Cedar Hill Ct Bedford 586-1105
Tuck's Tire & Auto Center Inc Moneta 297-5155
Turkey Mountain Greenhouses 586-0165
Tuscan Tavern pasta & Grill
  16483 Moneta Rd Moneta 297-8900
Two Nine Seven Minute market
  1110 E Main St Bedford 586-2546
Ty Davidson Well Drillikng
  1081 Jackson Hill Rd Bedford 586-5588

U

U-Haul Co 1123 Celebration Av Moneta 296-0507
U-Haul Co 13000 Moneta Rd 296-0656
U-Haul Neighborhood Dealer 2600 W Lynchburg
  Salem Tpke Bedford................................ 587-9443
U-Haul Neighborhood Dealer
  401 E Main St Bedford 586-5930
UPS 800-742-5877
US Cellular 888-289-8722
USPS 9161 Forest Rd Goode 586-4331
Unique Engineering Concepts Inc

  5700 Forest Rd Bedford 586-6761
United Country Atlantic Coast Auction & Realty Group
  309 E Main Bedford 586-0044
United States Government 586-4357
United States Government
  500 E Main St Bedford 586-5820
United States Government
  1031 Turnpike Rd Bedford 586-9646
United Support Services LLC
  102 N Bridge Bedford 586-1074
Unlimited Eletrical 6264 Forest Rd Bedford ... 586-8846
Unterbrink Thomas E Dr
  130 W Main St Bedford 586-3560
Updike Funeral Home
  11351 Leesville Rd Hudlstn 297-4966
Updike Funeral Home & Cremation Service
  1140 W Lynchburg Salem Trnpk Bedford 586-3304
  11351 Leesville Rd Hudlstn 297-4966
Updike Memorial
  1140 W Lynchburg Salem Trnpk Bedford 586-3304
Urologic Surgery PC 866-576-3045
Urologic Surgery PC 1802 Braeburn Dr Salem 444-4670
V
VEC Mercantile INC
  1035 Mercantile St Moneta 297-0967
Valley Core Drilling Inc Moneta 297-1573
Valley Oral Surgery PC Dr. Larry R. Meador
  4437 Starkey Rd Roanoke 774-5900
Valley View Consulting
  2428 Carter Mill Rd Hudlstn 297-3419
Verizon
Residential Services
New Service or Changes to Existing Service and Billing
Questions
Monday – Friday 8:00am-6:00pm
English 800-VERIZON 800 837-4966
Lunes a Viernes 8:00am a 6:00pm
Lunes a Viernes 8:00am a 6:00pm 800-VERIZON
800 837-4966
Chinese
Monday-Friday 8am-6pm EST 888 878-9188
Center for Customers with Disabilities Voice & TTY
Monday-Friday 8:30am-5:00pm 800-974-6006
Payment Information or Payment Arrangements
24 Hour Account Information
English
800-VERIZON 800-837-4966
informacion de cuentas disponible las 24 horas
Espanol 800-Verizon 800-837-4966
For Help Using Verizon
Products and Services 800-VERIZON 800-837-4966
Business Services
New Service or Changes to Existing Service and Billing
Questions
Monday-Friday 8:30am-5:00pm
English 800-826-2355
Lunes a Viernes 8:30am a 5:00pm
Espanol 800-483-4522
Payment Information or Payment Arrangements
24 Hour Account Information
English 800-599-0193
Informacion de cuentas disponible las 24 horas
Espanol 800-599-0193
Repair Services – 24 Hours
Residential Service 800-VERIZON 800-837-4966
Business Service 800-275-2355
Public Communications 800-822-2646

Continued – See next page

WEBSITE

Begin the timer and then scan the second part of the exercise for the answers to the following questions. As you find the answers, place them in the blank provided. When you are finished, immediately stop the timer and note the time in the space provided at the end of the questions. Grade your answers and put the number correct in the space provided below.

1. Which day does classes begin? _____

2. If I wanted to take an ICE (Institutional Challenge Exam), under which heading would I find it? _____

3. What is the email address for the Center for Academic Support and Advising Services (CASAS)? _____

4. How many departments are within CASAS? _____

5. Does CASAS have peer advising or professional advising? _____

6. Are the athletic advisors located within CASAS's Green Hall location? _____

7. Where would an engineering advisor be found? _____

8. What link would I use to locate the dean's name? _____

9. Can I pursue a Bachelor's degree in Applied Science in Technical Studies?

_____

10. New Student Orientation is connected to which department? _____

11. What is the physical address for CASAS? _____

12. If I am transferring in with good grades, what program could I investigate?

_____

13. Which academic program offers both a B.A. degree and a B.S. degree?

_____

14. As a math student, what entity might I consider visiting to enhance my learning style? _____

15. If I needed help with my resume/professional portfolio, which department would I likely visit?_____

16. For what group of students did an alumnus make a contribution?

_____

17. What is the CASAS phone number online students should use? _____

18. Under which heading would I look for information regarding Liberty SAT testing?

    _____

19. Which tab would I select, as a hearing impaired student, for assistance with my academic program? _____

20. Under which heading would I find information on the course catalog?

    _____

```
TIME:
NUMBER CORRECT:
```

Center for Academic Support and Advising Services

Departments

- Bruckner Learning Center
- Career Center
- Developmental Math
- Freshman Seminar & New Student Orientation
- Office Disability Academic Support
- Professional Advising
- Professional/ Continuing Education
- Tutoring/ Testing Center

Contact CASAS

casas@liberty.edu

Staff Listing

(434) 592-4110 (Resident)

(800) 424-9595 (Online)

(434) 582-2297

Location

CASAS has moved to a new location in Green Hall room 2668

›Directions to CASAS

›Map

**NCAA Athletes will still meet advisor in Williams Stadium
**SECS students will still meet advisor in Engineering Department

Academics

Majors
Individualized Studies (B.A., B.S)major

Interdisciplinary Studies (B.S.) major

Associate of Applied Science (A.A.S) in Technical Studies

Minors
Carpentry

Electrical

HVAC

Masonry

Plumbing

Welding

Honor Societies/Programs
Alpha Lambda Delta (freshman)

Eagle Scholars Program

Tua Sigma (transfer students)

Advising/Academic Resources
Advisor Contact Information

NCAA Student-Athlete Advising

Commonly Used Forms

Course Sequences

Declaration/Change of Major/Minor

Degree Completion Plans

Gen Ed/Intergrative Courses

Minors

New Student Information

CLEP Information

Course Catalog

ICE Exams

Special Academic Assistance

Programs

CASAS in the Media

Be Liberty - Academic Success (video)

Survival Kit - College Success (video)

Math Emporium Offers New Style of Learning

Virginia Technical Institute offers hands-on learning opportunities

Liberty to Host SAT tests

Alumnus contributes lab for special needs students

SENIOR CARE SERVICES

Begin the timer and then scan the second part of the exercise for the answers to the following questions. As you find the answers, place them in the blank provided. When you are finished, immediately stop the timer and note the time in the space provided at the end of the questions. Grade your answers and put the number correct in the space provided below.

1. If I lived in Bedford, which website would I visit to check out living facilities that would allow my elderly parent to retain some independence? _____

2. If I lived at 2100 Langhorne Road in Lynchburg and wanted to visit the home health care facility nearest me, which one would I choose? _____

3. Why would I consider the possibility that First Dominion and Personal Homecare, Inc. have the same owners? Be specific. _____

4. It appears that both hospitals in Lynchburg belong to the same corporation. What is the corporation name? _____

5. What number would I call in Madison Heights for information on home health care? _____

6. What facility in Lynchburg appears to be specifically for retired individuals?

    _____

7. If I were looking for nursing care for a senior citizen who wants to remain at home and lives on Fort Ave., which facility would I logically contact first?

    _____

8. Which facility in Bedford appears to be specifically for retired individuals?

    _____

9. Which website would I visit if I lived in Forest and was seeking information on adult day care? _____

10. Which phone number would I use in Madison Heights for home health care?

    _____

11. If I were seeking assistance with rehabilitation in a respite setting, which facility would I contact? _____

12. Which national organization has a housing option in the listing? _____

13. Which online address would I use to learn about home health care in Madison Heights? _____

14. Which facility appears to be part of a group for respite care? _____

15. Which city has **four** facilities under one corporate umbrella? _____

16. Which city has **three** facilities under one corporate umbrella? _____

17. Which senior housing facility in Amherst could you <u>not</u> research online?

_____

18. Which address is listed for the adult day care in Bedford apparently connected to the hospital? _____

19. If I lived on Amherst Hwy., which phone number could I call regarding home health care? _____

20. What adult daycare services appear to be connected with the Centra hospital system in Lynchburg? _____

```
TIME:
NUMBER CORRECT:
```

SENIOR CARE LISTING

CITY	NAME	ADDRESS	PHONE	WEB ADDRESS
REGIONAL HOUSING OPTIONS				
Amherst	Johnson Senior Center	108 & 112 Senior St.	434-946-2799	
Bedford	Campbell's Rest Home	1350 Longwood Ave.	540-586-0825	
Bedford	Elks National Home	931 Ashland Ave.	540-586-8232	www.elkshome.org
Lynchburg	Clear Brook Apts.	3004 Hill St.	434-845-2155	www.ClearBrook.org
Lynchburg	Jefferson House apts.	1818 Langhorne Rd.	434-846-1800	
Lynchburg	McGurk House	2425 Tate Springs Rd.	434-846-2425	www.McGurkHouse.org
ADULT DAY CARE SERVICES				
Bedford	Bedford Adult Day Care	1617 Oakwood St.	540-586-2441	www.bmhva.com
Bedford	Bedford Memorial Hospital	1613 Oakwood St.	540-586-8424	www.bmhva.com
Forest	Raspberry Hill	2617 Elk Valley Rd.	434-525-4422	www.RaspberryHillADC.com
Lynchburg	Centra PACE	407 Federal Street	434-200-6516	www.centrahealth.com
GERIATRIC CARE MANAGEMENT				
Lynchburg	CVAAA	501 12th Street	434-385-9070	www.cvaaa.com
Lynchburg	Infinity Care	21430 Timberlake Road	434-237-1975	www.infinitycare.org
HOSPITALS				
Bedford	Bedford Memorial Hospital	1613 Oakwood Street	540-586-2441	www.bmhva.org
Lynchburg	Centra Lynchburg General	2215 Landover Place	434-200-4000	www.lgh.centrahealth.com
Lynchburg	Centra Virginia Baptist	3300 Rivermont Ave.	434-947-4000	www.vbh.centrahealth.com
HOME HEALTH CARE				
Lynchburg	Amedisys Home Health	2050 Langhorne Road	434-845-7555	www.amedisys.com
Lynchburg	First Dominion	2808 Old Forest Road	434-384-2800	www.firstcare.biz
Lynchburg	Home Recovery of VA	5050 Fort Avenue	434-237-0021	http://hr-ha.com
Lynchburg	Interim Healthcare	2255 Langhorne Rd. Ste.6		
Lynchburg	Personal Homecare, Inc.	2808 Old Forest Rod.	434-384-2412	www.firstcare.biz
Lynchburg	Team Nurse	22634 Timberlake Rd. Ste. 6	434-832-7460	www.teamnurse.com
Madison Heights	Elite Care Services	5005 S. Amherst Hwy.	434-846-1514	www.EliteCareServicesLLC.com
ASSISTED LIV-ING FACILITIES				
Bedford	Carriage Hill Retirement	Roundtree Drive	540-586-5982	www.carriagehillretirement.com
Lynchburg	Bentley Commons	1604 Graves Mill Rd.	434-316-0207	www.bentleycommons.com/lynchburg
Lynchburg	The Oaks of Lynchburg	2249 Murrell Rd.	434-338-6882	www.springarborliving.com
Lynchburg	Valley View Retirement	1213 Long Meadows Rd.	434-237-3009	www.valleyviewretirement.com
Smith Mt. Lake	Runk & Pratt	115 Retirement Dr. Hardy	434-509-0087	www.runkandpratt.com
RESPITE CARE				
Appomattox	Appomattox Health and Rehabilitation	235 Evergreen Ave.	434-352-7420	www.lifeworksrehab.com
Lynchburg	Avante of Lynchburg	2081 Langhorne Rd.	434-846-8437	www.avantegroup.com
Lynchburg	Daybreak at Heritage Green	200 Lillian Lane	434-385-5102	www.heritagegreenal.com
Lynchburg	Runk & Pratt	20212 Leesville Road	434-237-7809	www.runkandpratt.com

CAR TABLE

Begin the timer and then scan the second part of the exercise for the answers to the following questions. As you find the answers, place them in the blank provided. Use ALL if a question is true of all models. When you are finished, immediately stop the timer and note the time in the space provided at the end of the questions. Grade your answers and put the number correct in the space provided below.

Models with the following features...

1. Roof Rails
2. Hard Disk Drive
3. Bluetooth
4. XM Radio
5. Security System
6. Passive Safety Features
7. Child-Proof Rear Door Locks
8. Power Tailgate
9. Black Body-Colored Power Side Mirrors
10. Body-Colored Parking Sensors
11. Integrated Trailer Hitch with Trailer Harness
12. Fog Lights
13. 21.0 Fuel EPA Mileage Rating
14. Available DVD Rear Entertainment System
15. HomeLink Remote System
16. Integrated Sunshades (2nd row)
17. Front and 2nd-Row Floor Mats Only
18. Heated (4WD)-Body Colored Power Side Mirrors
19. Required Fuel: Regular Unleaded
20. Available Honda Satellite-Linked Navigation System

1. _____
2. _____
3. _____
4. _____
5. _____
6. _____
7. _____
8. _____
9. _____
10. _____
11. _____
12. _____
13. _____
14. _____
15. _____
16. _____
17. _____
18. _____
19. _____
20. _____

TIME:
NUMBER CORRECT:

CAR MODEL INFORMATION

ENGINEERING	LX	EX	EX-L	Touring
Engine Type	V-6	V-6	V-6	V-6
Displacement (cc)	3471	3471	3471	3471
Horsepower @ rpm (SAE net)/Torque (lb-ft @rpm, SAE net)	250 @ 5700/253 @4800	250 @ 5700/253 @4800	250 @ 5700/253 @4800	250 @ 5700/253 @4800
Valve Train	24-Valve SOHC i-VTEC©	24-Valve SOHC i-VTEC©	24-Valve SOHC i-VTEC©	24-Valve SOHC i-VTEC©
Drive-by-Wire Throttle System	•	•	•	•
Variable Cylinder Management TM (VCM©)	•	•	•	•
Active Noise Cancellation TM	•	•	•	•
Hill Start Assist	•	•	•	•
Variable Torque Management© 4-Wheel-Drive System (VTM-4©)	Available	Available	Available	Available
CARB Emissions Rating ©	ULEV-2	ULEV-2	ULEV-2	ULEV-2
Heavy-Duty Radiator with 160-Watt Fans (2)	•	•	•	•
Heavy-Duty Power-Steering-Fluid Cooler	•	•	•	•
TRANSMISSION				
5-Speed Automatic Transmission	•	•	•	•
Heavy-Duty Automatic-Transmission-Fluid Cooler	4WD models	4WD models	4WD models	4WD models
BODY/SUSPENSION/CHASSIS				
MacPherson Strut Front Suspension/Multi-Link Rear Suspension with Trailing Arms	•	•	•	•
Power-Assisted Ventilated Front Disc/Solid Rear Disc Brakes (in)	13.0/13.1	13.0/13.1	13.0/13.1	13.0/13.1
Wheels/Tires	17" Steel/ P235/65 R17 108T	18" Alloy/ P235/60 R18 102T	18" Alloy/ P235/60 R18 102T	18" Alloy/ P235/60 R18 102T
EPA MILEAGE RATINGS/FUEL				
5-Speed Automatic (2WD; City/Highway/ Combined)	18/25/21	18/25/21	18/25/21	18/25/21
5-Speed Automatic (4WD; City/Highway/ Combined)	17/24/20	17/24/20	17/24/20	17/24/20
Fuel (gal)	21.0	21.0	21.0	21.0
Required Fuel	Regular Unleaded	Regular Unleaded	Regular Unleaded	Regular Unleaded
ACTIVE SAFETY				
Vehicle Stability Assist ™ (VSA©) with Traction Control and Brake Assist	•	•	•	•
Anti-Lock Braking System (ABS) with Electronic Brake Distribution (EBD)	•	•	•	•
Tire Pressure Monitoring System (TPMS) 10	•	•	•	•
Daytime running Lights (DRL)	•	•	•	•
PASSIVE SAFETY				
Advanced Compatibility Engineering ™ (ACE ™) Body Structure	•	•	•	•
Dual-Stage, Multiple-Threshold Front Airbags (SRS)	•	•	•	•
Front Side Airbags with Passenger-Side Occupant Position Detection System (OPDS)	•	•	•	•

PASSIVE SAFETY	LX	EX	EX-L	Touring
Three-Row Side Curtain Airbags with Rollover Sensor	•	•	•	•
Driver's and Front Passenger's Active Head Restraints	•	•	•	•
3-Point Seat Belts at all Seating Positions	•	•	•	•
Front 3-Point Seat Belts with Automatic Tensioning System	•	•	•	•
Lower Anchors and Tethers for Children (LATCH): Lower Anchors (2nd-Row All, 3rd-Row Passenger Side), Tether Anchors (2nd-Row All, 3rd-Row All)	•	•	•	•
Driver's and Front Passenger's Seat-Belt Reminder	•	•	•	•
Child-Proof Rear Door Locks	•	•	•	•
EXTERIOR FEATURES				
One-Touch Power Moonroof with Tilt Feature			•	•
Tailgate with Lift-Up Glass Hatch	•	•	with Power Tailgate	with Power Tailgate
Remote Entry	•	•	•	•
Security System		•	•	•
Body-Colored Power Side Mirrors	Black	Heated (4WD)	Heated (4WD)	Heated (4WD) with Memory and Integrated Turn Indicators
Acoustic Windshield	•	•	•	•
Rear Privacy Glass	•	•	•	•
Integrated Class III Trailer Hitch/Pre-Wired for Trailer Harness	•	•	•	Includes Trailer Harness
Roof Rails				•
Fog Lights		•	•	•
Multi-Reflector Halogen Headlights with Auto-Off	•	with Auto-On/Off	with Auto-On/Off	with Auto-On/Off
Body-Colored Parking Sensors (front/rear)				•
COMFORT & CONVENIENCE				
Tri-Zone Automatic Climate Control System with Humidity Control and Air Filtration	•	•	•	•
Honda Satellite-Linked Navigation System™ with Voice Recognition, FM Traffic, Multi-Angle Rearview Camera with Guidelines and Compass			Available	•
i-MID with 8-Inch High-Resolution WVGA (800x480) Screen, Customizable Feature Settings and Interface Dial			with Navigation	•
i-MID with 8-Inch WQVGA (480x320) Screen, Customizable Feature Settings and Rearview Camera with Guidelines	•	•	without Navigation	
Honda DVD Rear Entertainment System			Available	•
Bluetooth© 7 HandsFreeLink©	•	•	•	•
Power Windows with Auto-Up/Down Driver's and Front Passenger's Window	•	•	•	•
Power Door and Tailgate Locks	•	•	•	•
Cruise Control	•	•	•	•
Leather-Wrapped Steering Wheel			•	•
HomeLink©12 Remote System		•	•	•

COMFORT & CONVENIENCE	LX	EX	EX-L	Touring
Illuminated Steering Wheel-Mounted Controls	Cruise/ Audio/ Phone	Cruise/ Audio/Phone	Cruise/Au- dio/Phone/ Navigation (available)	Cruise/Audio/ Phone/Naviga- tion
Multi-Functional Center Control Storage	•	•	•	•
Tilt and Telescopic Steering Column	•	•	•	•
12-Volt Power Outlets (Front, 2nd-Row and Cargo Area)	•	•	•	•
115-Volt Power Outlet (Center Console)			with RES	•
Map Lights (All Rows)	•	•	•	•
Ambient Console Lighting	•	•	•	•
Integrated Sunshades (2nd-Row)				•
Floor Mats	Front and 2nd-Row	Front and 2nd-Row	Front and 2nd-Row	All Rows
Hidden Storage Well	•	•	•	•
SEATING				
Driver's Seat with 10-Way Power Adjustment, Including Power Lumbar Support		•	•	with Two-Position Memory
Passenger's Seat with 4-Way Power Adjustment			•	•
Leather-Trimmed Interior/Heated Front Seats			•	•
60/40 Split, Flat-Folding, Sliding, and Reclining 2nd-Row Bench Seat	•	•	•	•
60/40 Split, Flat-Folding 3rd-Row Bench Seat	•	•	•	•
AUDIO SYSTEMS				
229-Watt AM/FM/CD Audio System with 7 Speakers, Including Subwoofer	•	•	without Navigation	
246-Watt AM/FM/CD Audio System with 7 Speakers, Including Subwoofer			with Navigation	
650-Watt AM/FM/CD Premium Audio System with 10 Speakers, Including Subwoofer				•
Hard Disk Drive (HDD)5 with 15-GB Audio Memory/Song By Voice© (SBV)			with Navigation	
2-GB CD Library	•	•	without Navigation	
XM© Radio 13			•	•
USB Audio Interface©	•	•	•	•
Bluetooth7 Streaming Audio	•	•	•	•
MP3/Auxiliary Input Jack	•	•	•	•

AMTRAK SCHEDULE

Begin the timer and then scan the second part of the exercise for the answers to the following questions. As you find the answers, place them in the blank provided. Answer with entry as exactly noted in schedule; also, use number symbols (1, 2, 3, etc.) rather than number words (one, two, etc.). When you are finished, immediately stop the timer and note the time in the space provided at the end of the questions. Grade your answers and put the number correct in the space provided below.

1. How many stations have 5 or more amenities? _____

2. Which station has no address indicated? _____

3. Which station has the code HMW? _____

4. How many stations have limited wheelchair accessibility? _____

5. Which station has the following address:

   BP Station, 130 N. Ensley St., 49329? _____

6. Which station is located in Canada? _____

7. How many stations may or may not be open for all train departures? _____

8. How many stations have Wi-Fi capabilities? _____

9. Which station can you find on pages 108, 109, and 111, etc.? _____

10. On which pages can you find details about services? _____

11. On this schedule, Hollywood is in which state? _____

12. Which state has the most listings? _____

13. How many stations have bus stops as denoted by the bus icon? _____

14. Service has been suspended between _____ and New Orleans.

15. How many listings are on page 71? _____

16. How many stations are in Nebraska? _____

17. How many stations does UT have? _____

18. How many cities have a name ending in "....burg"? _____

19. Which station name do MD and MI have in common? _____

20. The listing with page numbers 54-57, 60, and 61 has how many amenities? _____

```
TIME:
NUMBER CORRECT:
```

AMTRAK STATION OR BUS STOP	PAGE NO.	CODE	AMENITIES
GREENSBORO, NC 236 E. Washington St., 27401	64,66,68	GRO	🚆 ● ○ 🧳 ♿ QT
GREENSBURG, PA Harrions Ave. and Seton Hill Dr., 15601	50-53, 70	GNB	🚆 ○
GREENFIELD VILLAGE, MI 20900 Oakwood Blvd., 48216 Special Stop-See Note 63 (for Group Travel)	76	GFV	🚆 ○
GREENSVILLE, NC Greenville Area Transit Transfer Center, Second and Reeds Sts. 27834	64	GRN	🚌 ○ ♿
GREENSVILLE, SC 1120 W. Washington St., 29601	66	GRV	🚆 ● 🧳 ♿
GREENWOOD, MS 506 Carrolton Ave. (Carrolton Ave. and E. Gibson St.), 38930	79	GWD	🚆 ○ ♿
GRIMSBY, ON Ontario St. and Drake Ave., L3M 3H6	54-57, 131	GMS	🚆 ○ 🍁
GROVER BEACH, CA 180 W. Grand Ave., 93433	108, 109, 111, 117, 124-127	GVB	🚆 ○ 🚌 ♿ QT
GUADALUPE/SANTA MARIA, CA (See ALSO SANTA MARIA, CA) 330 Guadalupe St. (Hwy 1), Guadalupe, 93434	108, 109, 124-127	GUA	🚆 QT ○ ♿
GULFPORT, MS	*		
HAGERSTOWN, MD MTA Park 'n Ride, 18306 Colonel H. K. Douglas Dr., 21740	31,41	HAG	🚌 ○
HAMLET, NC 2 Main St., 28345	64	HAM	🚆 QT ○ ♿
HAMMOND, LA 404 N. E. Railroad Ave., 70401	79	HMD	🚆 ● 🧳 ♿
HAMMOND-WHITING, IN 1135 N. Calcumet Ave., Hammond, 46320	76	HMI	🚆 ○ ♿
HAMMONTON, NJ New Jersey Transit Station, Egg Harbour Rd. and Line St. 08037	49	HTN	🚆 ○
HANCOCK, MD Hancock Truck Plaza, 434 E. Main St., 21750	31, 41	HNK	🚌 ○
HANCOCK, MI Shottle Bop Liquor Store, 125 Quincy St., 49930	85	HKM	🚌 ○
HANFORD, CA 200 Santa Fe Ave. #A, 93230	111, 114, 115	HNF	🚆 🚌 🧳 ♿ ◑ QT

AMTRAK STATION OR BUS STOP	PAGE NO.	CODE	AMENITIES
HARPERS FERRY, WV Potomac and Shenandoah Sts., 25425	72	HFY	
HARRISBURG, PA 4th and Chestnut Sts., 17101	50-53, 70, 72	HAR	
HARTFORD, CT One Union Place, 06103	27-45, 67	HFD	
HASTINGS, NE 501 W. First St., 68901	91	HAS	
HATTIESBURG, MS 308 Newman St., 39401	66	HBG	
HAVERHILL, MA Washington St. at Railroad Square, 01832	46, 47	HHL	
HAVLOCK, NC Tourism and Event Center, 201 Tourist Center Dr., 28532	64	HVL	
HAVRE, MT 235 Maint St., 59501	88	HAV	
HAYWARD, CA 22555 Meekland Ave., 94541	108, 109, 116-121	HAY	
HAZLEHURST, MS N. Ragsdale Ave. and E. Conway St., 39083	79	HAZ	
HEALDSBURG, CA Singletree Inn, 165 Healdsburg Ave., 95448	111	HEA	

AMTRAK STATION OR BUS STOP	PAGE NO.	CODE	AMENITIES
HELPER, UT 1 Depot St., 84526	91	HER	🚌 ○ ▦
HEMET, CA Simpson Senior Center, 305 E. Devonshire Ave., 92543 Coco's Restaurant, 3246 W. Florida Ave., 92545	110, 110	HMT HET	🚌 ○ ♿ 🚌 ○
HERMANN, MO Wharf and Gutenburg Sts., 65041	80, 81	HEM	🚌 ○ ♿
HIGH POINT, NC 100 W. High Ave., 27260	64, 66, 68	HPT	🚌 ◑ ♿ *QT*
HINCKLEY, MN Tobie's Restaurant, 404 Fire Monument Rd., I-35 & Hwy. 48, 55037	89	HKL	🚌 ○
HINTON, WV Front St. and Fifth Ave., 25951	71	HIN	🚌 ○
HOLDREGE, NE 100 West Ave., 68949	91	HLD	🚌 ○ ♿
HOLLAND, MI 171 Lincoln Ave., 49423	78	HOM	🚌 ○ ♿ *QT*
HOLLYWOOD, FL 3001 Hollywood Blvd., 33021	65	HOL	🚌 ● ♿ 🧳 *QT*
HOMEWOOD, IL 18015 Park Ave., 60430	79	HMW	🚌 ● *QT*
HOOD RIVER, OR 114 Cascade Ave., curbside stop adjacent to the Eye- glass Store, 97031	102	HOO	🚌 ○
HOPE, AR 100 E. Division St., 71801	94	HOP	🚌 ○ ♿
HOUGHTON, MI Memorial Union Building (Michigan Tech), 49931	85	HGH	🚌 ○
HOUSTON, TX 902 Washington Ave., 77002	95, 96	HOS	🚌 ● ♿ 🧳 🚌
HOWARD CITY, MI BP Station, 130 N. Ensley St., 49329	77	HWC	🚌 ○ ♿
HUDSON, NY 69 S. Front St., 12534	54-57, 60, 61	HUD	🚌 ● ♿ *QT*
HUNTINGDON, PA 4th and Allegheny Sts. 16652	50-53, 70	HGD	🚌 ○
HUNTINGTON, WV 1050 8th. Ave., 25701	71	HUN	🚌 ● 🧳 ♿

AMTRAK STATION OR BUS STOP	PAGE NO.	CODE	AMENITIES
HUTCHINSON, KS N. Walnut St. and E. 3rd Ave., 67501	92	HUT	🚆 ◯ ♿
INDEPENDENCE, MO 600 S. Grand Ave., 64050	80, 81	IDP	🚆 ◯
INDIANAPOLIS, IN 350 S. Illinios St., 46225	71, 72, 83	IND	🚆 🚌 ● ♿ 🧳 *QT*
INDIO, CA Behind Denny's Restaurant, northeast corner, Hwy. 111 at Monroe St., 92201	110, 125	IDO	🚌 ◯ ♿
Irvine, CA Transportation Center, 15215 Barranca Pkwy., 92618	97, 108, 109, 114, 115, 124-127	IRV	🚆 🚌 ● 🧳 *QT*
ISLETON, CA Delta Breeze Transit stop, 100 2nd St., 95641	123	ISE	🚌 ◯
JACKSON, MI 501 E. Michigan Ave., 49201	76	JXN	🚆 🚌 ● ♿ *QT*
JACKSON, MS 300 W. Capitol St., 39201	79	JAN	🚆 🧳 ● ♿ *QT*
JACKSONVILLE, FL 3570 Clifford Lane, 32209	65, 72, 96	JAX	🚆 🧳 ● ♿ *QT*
JACKSONVILLE, NC Next to Hess Gas Station, 850 New Bridge St., 28540	64	JNC	🚌 ◯ ♿
JAMESTOWN, NY US News Agency, 111 W. Third St., 14701	54, 56	JMN	🚌 ◯
JANESVILLE, WI Bus Station, 3120 N. Pontiac Dr., 53545	83	JVL	🚌 ◯

 Wi-fi available on train

 Staffed Station with ticket office; may or may not be open for all train departures

 Station wheelchair accesible; no barriers between station and train

 Station wheelchair accessible; not all station facilities accessible

The Sunset Limited service between Orlando and New Orleans has been suspended. Future service has not been determined.

Details about our services
see pages 131-144

SCANNING ANSWER KEYS

1. Alphabetical Listing of Animals

1. Crustaceans (s) 2. Bandicoot 3. Blue Whale 4. Hippopotamus
5. Iguanodon 6. Galapagos Tortoise 7. Eurasian Lynx 8. Aye-Aye
9. Hairy-nosed Wombat 10. Dugong 11. Galagpagos Land Iguana
12. Hare Harp Seal 13. Beluga Whale 14. Coral(s) and Anemone(s)
15. Chinchilla 16. Gibbon 17. Aardvark 18. Capybara
19. Irrawaddy Dolphin 20. Bonobo

2. Alphabetical Listing of Dinosaurs

1. Balaur 2. Abelisaurus 3. Edmarka 4. Efraasia 5. Cerasinops
6. Ceratonykus 7. Eodromaeus 8. Anatosaurus 9. Amazonsaurus
10. Chilantaisaurus 11. Bactrosaurus 12. Camarasaurus 13. Alamosaurus
14. Epidendrosaurus 15. Dacentrurus 16. Bruhathkayosaurus 17. Dromaeosaurus
18. Alxasaurus 19. Chialingosaurus 20. Carcharodontosaurus

3. Alphabetical Listing Renaissance Artists

1. da Forli, Melozzo 2. Cariani, Giovanni 3. Daddi, Bernardo 4. Bellini, Gentile
5. Andrea, Zoan 6. Cazzaniga, Tommaso 7. Blondeel, Lancelot 8. David, Gerard
9. Bergognone 10. Congnet, Gillis 11. Dalmata, Giovanni 12. Brusasorci
13. Claeissens I, Peter 14. Aertsen, Pieter 15. Da Modena, Giovanni
16. Cozzarelli, Guidoccio 17. Bambaia 18. Bregno, Andrea
19. Binck, Jacob 20. Daret, Jacques

4. State Government Directory

1. 6 2. 6 3. 34-46 4. Financial Accounting & Reporting Section
5. Kanawha 6. Health and Human Resources 7. 3 8. Division of Labor
9. 13 10. 2 11. Consolidated Public Retirement Board
12. Public Employees Grievance Board 13. 3 14. 26
15. 32 16. 27, 29 17. Criminal Law Research
18. Public 19. MERCER 20. 2

5. Notary Public Application

1. 60 2. No 3. False 4. $5.00 5. July 1 6. False 7. Commonwealth 8. Outside
9. False 10. Identity 11. True 12. Expire 13. Initialed 14. Notary 15. False

16. Public   17. Perjury   18. False   19. False   20. Third

6. Parks and Recreation Table

1. Blackwater Creek Natural Area   2. Five   3. Riverfront Park   4. Peaks View Park
5. One   6. Peaks View Park   7. Miller Park   8. Peaks View Park   9. Below 25 ft.
10. None   11. Three   12. Nine   13. Miller Park   14. None   15. Natural Area
16. 315 Chambers St.   17. Valleyview Playlot 18. Westover Neighborhood Park
19. Heritage Park   20. Miller Park

7. Football Roster

1. VA   2. 12   3. Kyle DeArmon   4. 14   5. 12   6. 3   7. 9   8. 2   9. 3   10. 49
11. Florida (12)   12. 13   13. Ryan Greiser   14. SC   15. 23   16. No
17. Matt Camire 18. 29   19. Monroe, NC   20. 2

8. Aquatics Lessons Schedule

1. 9:55-10:40 AM   2. Miller Park Pool   3. $55   4. 7/8-7/18   5. 30-45 minutes
6. 7/8 - 7/18   7. 34010.206   8. 6:30-7:00   9. Wednesday   10. American Red Cross
11. 6/17-6/27   12. 16 years & up   13. Mon-Thurs   14. Eight   14. Eight
15. 7:05-7:45 pm   16. Fridays   17. 18 months-3 yrs.   18. 7/29-8/8   19. $40
20. 34013.203

9. Physicians Registry

1. Dr. Trudy Shahady   2. Mitchell Hodges
3. Blue Ridge Ear, Nose, Throat & Plastic Surgery   4. Kathy Worley
5. Dr. C. Michael Valentine   6. www.gastrocentralva.com   7. 22
8. Ms. Carolyn Bagley   9. Dr. Mark Townsend   10. Ms. Phyllis Everett
11. Ms. Mary Sue Ramey   12. 4262 South Amherst Highway,   Madison Heights, VA
24572   13. (434) 332-7367   14. www.cvfp.net   15. Dr. Leah Hinkle, M.D.
16. Alan B. Pearson Regional Cancer Center   17. Dr. Johanna Brown
18. Timberlake Family Practice   19. Dr. Patricia Powers   20. Dr. Robert Elliott

10. Telephone Directory

1. 1 Mountain View Rd, Lynchburg   2. 800-526-1177   3. 297-1233   4. 888-878-9188
5. Shrader Engineering and Land Surveying, Inc.   6. 800-634-7928   7. 15388 Moneta Rd.
8. Cheryl Z. Saville   9. Dr. Larry R. Meador   10. 800-275-2355   11. 800-572-3303
12. 586-5820 13. 1433 E. Main St., Bedford 14. 297-1597

15. www.bankoffincastle.com   16. 800-837-4966 17. 1802 Braeburn Drive, Salem
18. Tharp Funeral Home and Crematory 19. 116 S. Bridge Street, Bedford
20. 800-854-8965

11. Website

1. August 19 2. Advising/Academic Resources 3. casas@liberty.edu 4. Eight
5. Professional Advising   6. No 7. Engineering Department 8. Staff Listing 9. No
10. Freshman Seminar & New Student Orientation   11. Green Hall room 2668
12.   Tau Sigma 13. Individualized Studies 14. Math Emporium   15. Career Center
16. special needs   17. (800) 424-9595   18. CASAS in the Media
19. Office of Disability Academic Support   20. Advising/Academic Support

12. Senior Care Services Table

1. www.carrriagehillretirement.com   2. Interim Healthcare
3. Same website www.firstcare.biz   4. Centra 5. 434-846-1514
6. Valley View Retirement   7. Home Recovery of VA   8. Carriage Hill Retirement
9. www.RaspberryHillADC.com 10. 434-846-1514
11. Appomattox Health and Rehabilitation 12. Elks National Home
13. www.EliteCareServicesLLC.com 14. Avante of Lynchburg 15. Lynchburg
16. Bedford   17. Johnson Senior Center   18. 1616 Oakwood St.   19. 434-846-1514
20. Centra PACE

13. Car Table

1. Touring   2. Ex-L and Touring   3. All   4. Ex-L, Touring   5. Ex, Ex-L, Touring
6. All   7. All   8. Ex-L, Touring   9. LX   10. Touring   11. Touring   12. Ex, Ex-L,
Touring   13. All   14. Ex-L   15. Ex, Ex-L, Touring   16. Touring   17. LX, Ex, Ex-L
18. Ex, Ex-L, Touring   19. All   20. Ex-L

14. Amtrack Schedule

1. 10 2. Gulfport, MS 3. Homewood, IL 4. 15   5. Howard City, MI 6. Grimsby, ON
7. 17 8. None 9. Grover Beach, Ca 10. 131-144   11. FL   12. CA/23   13.17
14. Orlando 15. 3   16. 2 17. 1   18. 4 19. Hancock 20. 4

CPSIA information can be obtained at www.ICGtesting.com
Printed in the USA
LVOW03s0245290615

444236LV00014B/218/P